CALL ME

Skybabe™

CALL ME
Skybabe™

**The Unfiltered, Laugh-Out-Loud,
Empowering Guide to Finding Your Way to
Health, Love, and Joy While Flying**

TEE R. & NENA O.

For you, *Skybabe*.

The extraordinary soul who knows more than she says, thinks more than she speaks, and notices more than others realize.

May you find love, happiness, and peace in every corner of the world.

A mile of highway will take you just one mile, but a
mile of runway will take you
ANYWHERE!
Unknown

Contents

Skybabe,

During the first global lockdown in March 2020, when the entire world turned upside down, we couldn't sit with our hands crossed. While we kept our bodies active by going up and down the stairs for an infinite number of times, we had to keep our minds busy. So, we decided to write.

Every day, between 11 a.m. and one o'clock in the afternoon, we'd sit at our desks and type away. Sometimes together over a Zoom call, sometimes alone—amid chaos, online learning, and screaming into a pillow—we still did it.

We've all been there. Literally the whole freaking world went through a horrific time in history that changed our lives forever. The pandemic has resulted in lockdowns and travel restrictions in every corner of our beautiful Earth. This had a major impact on the global aviation industry, leaving hundred thousand of our colleagues and their families without jobs. Leaving travelers stranded and all those who have an itch for travel alone and devastated. So, if there's one lesson this pandemic taught us, it's to never delay our dreams.

We all have a limited time on this blue planet and we're not wasting a second of it.

While we wanted to include all our experiences in this book, it just didn't seem like a smart idea. We wanted this book to be a relaxing, fast-paced, and laugh-out-loud guide that will come in handy for any *Skybabe* out there—the one who is already flying or has retired, the one who is thinking of flying, and the one who is curious to learn more and simply wants to have fun with us. So, after careful consideration and strenuous editing, we decided to leave many chapters and topics out.

You didn't come here to read *War and Peace*, did you, *Skybabe*? Yep, we thought so.

The stories are interconnected and may sometimes seem alike, but they're just our personal experiences. While most of the time you'll know who's writing, sometimes it will be unclear. And that's because we want you to think of us as one *Skybabe*.

So, why us and who the heck are we to tell you anything?

While you can learn more about us in the About the Authors section, here, we're just going to mention a few things.

Together, we flew across the Earth over 400 times, spent nearly 20,000 hours on the plane, packed over thirteen million miles in our suitcases, and visited two-thirds of this wonderful planet. And, we flew on some of the biggest passenger aircraft today: Airbus A330-300, Airbus A340-500/800, Airbus A380, and Boeing 777-200/300 ER, taking care of gazillions of customers.

With over 20 years in aviation, we bring you a journey through the skies while helping you learn how to take care of yourself and preserve your health and well-being while flying.

The journey you are about to embark on has the power to change you. And if you allow it, it *will* change you.

As journaling masters who have been jotting their thoughts for several decades, we're here to tell you that each time you travel to a new place, you gain something that stays with you forever. Something no one can take away from you, something that is worth living for while experiencing life in the most magnificent way. And you get to write it all down as you go along. That's why we also created the super cute *Skybabe* Journal that fits perfectly in your bag so it can travel with you wherever you go.

But before we share our story with you, be warned:

Yes, flying is amazing. It lets you see the world, learn about new places, meet incredible people, and indulge in different cultures. But while it brings all the amazing experiences, it's not always what you would expect. Flying can be uncomfortable. It can tear you apart and even leave you heartbroken. It can bring out the worst and definitely the best in you. And that's fine. Perfectly fine. Because it is all part of the process—the journey you are on that helps you grow and overcome fears and doubts you avoided for so long.

Now that we have that sorted out, let's get this show on the road.

With love,

Tee & Nena

In the land of the seven sands, in the city we proudly call our home, on this 22nd day of February, 2022.

Who Is Skybabe?

Once you have tasted flight, you will forever walk the
earth with your eyes turned skyward, for there you
have been, and there you will always long to return.
Leonardo da Vinci

Skybabe is a feminine, curious, spiritual soul, eager to explore the
world, absorb different cultures, and meet and get to know people
from all around. She's happy, healthy, and fulfilled. She knows what
she wants, and she is aligned with her vision, dreams and goals, and
even when things don't go as planned, she knows herself so well
to handle any situation for her own good. She takes care of herself,
her health, her finances, her inner world, and the environment. She
cares for others and she selflessly gives when her help is needed.

Skybabe likes to read — everything from fairytales and history
books to personal development success stories. It's not rare to see
her open up a cookbook, too.

Skybabe loves music and movement. She is an empath and a
sensitive soul. She is caring and likes to help others. She stays
away from fake conversations, arguments, and inauthentic people.
She is courageous and bold. She likes to put herself out of her

comfort zone, whether by traveling somewhere alone, trying new peculiar dishes, or hopping on new adventures. She likes to spend time meditating and counting her blessings. She is a cheerful and positive spirit, who sees the good in every situation.

Skybabe has big dreams and takes inspired action to achieve them daily. She loves money and sees it as an indispensable energy that comes to her easily, effortlessly, and abundantly. As much as she uses money to make her life beautiful, she utilizes it to support others and help them achieve their goals and dreams.

She travels freely and finds pieces of herself wherever she goes. With each trip and each story, she becomes a bit more of who she is. Even if she's still searching for the meaning of her existence, she knows she's the one who holds everything in her hands—her future, her dreams, her love life. She travels to find herself and be a little more of who she really is with each trip she takes. She is accomplished, cheerful, and giving.

Skybabe is of service, and a great example of a person who can integrate life and work well. She is beautiful, inspired, motivated, wealthy, healthy, knowledgeable, and loving toward herself and others. *Skybabe* is willing to learn and develop. She is self-driven, mindful, respectful, and respected.

HOW MANY HATS DO YOU WEAR, *SKYBABE,* OR WHAT DO YOU *ACTUALLY* DO?

Let's see . . .

I'm a hostess. I welcome hundreds of passengers aboard every flight. I pronounce their names with ease because I've read thousands and thousands so far. Everything from Mr. Bhattacharyya and Mrs. Poh to Mrs. Vishwanath and Mrs. Splettstoesser. I smile at each one of them and give them a warm welcome. And yes, we're going to Thiruvananthapuram today.

I'm a nurse and a midwife. I tend to different kinds of injuries, sicknesses, and medical issues. I provide oxygen like giving a piece of gum for fresh breath. I take care of sick passengers, pregnant women, and the elderly. I deliver babies to this world in-flight, and take care of mothers in those special moments.

I'm a first responder. I give CPR and save lives.

I'm a counselor. I reassure people and talk to them about their problems. I comfort the ones who just lost a loved one and are on their way home to bury them. Yes, I cry with them, too.

I'm a conflict-resolution manager. I help couples reconcile. I help passengers settle an argument. I work out any differences between my crew members. Sometimes it ain't pretty, but someone's gotta do it.

I'm a mother. I take care of babies and children. I talk to them. I play with them. I sing to them. I give them toys. I soothe them when they cry restlessly, to give their mommas a tiny break to sleep and rest. I also look after minors traveling on their own. Under my watchful hawk's eye, nothing gets unnoticed, so those kids are safe to travel with me.

I'm a carer of the elderly. I assist them with their bags, help them go to the toilet, bring them food, open it up, get it ready. I carry and pull wheelchairs through the aisle and take the disabled passengers to the toilet. I wipe the toilet seat with a wet wipe and cover it with a seat cover.

I'm a psychotherapist. I deal with anxieties and phobias, but most frequently, the common fear of flying.

I'm a physician. I communicate with the doctors on the ground and act like one in the air. I provide medications, take health history, write reports. I save lives.

I'm a salesperson. I sell Duty Free items and onboard upgrades.

I'm an accountant and a quality control executive. I have to be precise and always count well, with all the time restrictions, number and types of meals, and meal service requirements.

I'm a security officer. I take care of all the people we accept on board and make sure they are safe to fly with us. I use my observation and judgment. I have eyes in the back of my head and I hear everything. Nothing surprises me. Because I know my life is as valuable as anyone else's on board that flight.

I'm a server and a waitress. I serve food—the famous chicken or beef & tea or coffee. In First Class, I offer the best on-demand service there is. I am resourceful and find solutions to any problem I possibly can.

I'm *Skybabe* and, heck, I ain't ashamed to say it. I get to see the world doing it ALL.

1

Let That Bubble Burst

BLOATED TUMMY OF VIOLETS AND ROSES

Nothing is more conspicuous than a farting princess.
Jack Vance

I'm standing at the open passenger door. Boarding is about to start. Full makeup, spotless uniform, immaculate grooming. I look like a million-dollar babe. I _feel_ like one. Totally rocking this moment until my rumbling tummy threatens to ruin my reputation.

Oh, God! If only that toilet were nearer.

Being a sprint racer in heels would be a superb skill to have right now.

I turn to my right with my heart thumping in my chest. The sweat trickling down my back reminds me that this is all very real. The zealous crowd of eager passengers marches toward me.

Think, gurrrl, think! Think goddamn it!

If I add a bit of speed to my pace, I could be in that lavatory in a matter of seconds, and finally release the bursting bubble that's been building in me.

Do I call a colleague? Do I just leave the door and disappear?

Hell, no. I'm the senior here. I'm the person my junior colleagues look up to. I can't. Uh-uh, no way!

But shit's getting serious. My mind is playing tricks on me, and I know I should have listened to my brain, not my gut. You had to have not one, but two bubble teas in Taipei. Your greedy peepers, hungrier than grizzly's eyes during salmon spawning season, deceived you. Again. And now you regret the moment you *slurrrrrrrrped* those last few drops of the delicious boba pearls that brought you right where you are now.

This boarding lasts forever. I wish I could, but I cannot jump over passengers' heads. That would be really stupid.

Oh, well ... *pffffffffffft*

It's out. The deed is done. Violets and roses blossomed. And right in front of an entire army of people.

Great! Just great!

Shame will eat me alive.

And just when the moment's right, I see the cute Argentinian colleague coming my way. As the tall handsome silhouette approaches me, his strong masculine cologne invades my nostrils and, for a moment, I sigh a breath of relief.

But no. Even the strongest perfume can't cover the beautiful new feminine fragrance line I created a few seconds ago.

Let this planet swallow me *now*.

There's no escape. He is here already. I stick my nose up in the air, look left and right and start sniffing like an eager dog let loose on a new, unknown walkway. With a sour face, I quickly comment on the disgusting smell surrounding us, expressing my disbelief and wonder of its mysterious origin. He nods, pinches his nostrils tightly, swings around, pivoting on his feet as a proper tango dancer would, and leaves swiftly, without forgetting to say, *"Puta madre!"*

The air has just cleared. Well, not literally, because it still stank, but the path between the seats emptied, and I darted to the toilet, almost falling over a passenger's bag. Nearly there. Yes, yes, just a few more steps.

Mierda! My heel's stuck! Could this day get any worse?

I pull my leg out and shove my shoulders through the door, pushing it with all my might. Finally! I'm in the lavatory. My sanctuary. The place of complete peace and calm. Safe from prying eyes and curious sniffers, farting my shame away with the concerto of trumpets, trombones, and bugles. *Ahh.*

Skybabe, have you ever experienced that awkward moment when you had to hold it while locked in that tube in the air and couldn't go just about anywhere to release it? All the while surrounded by a herd of people?

I don't even have to hear you say it because I know it! Been there, done that. So many times. And I empathize with you sincerely, *Skybabe.*

What a constricting feeling! The skirt, the trousers, the belt, the pantyhose! Whatever you have on. You name it. Every single thing, even the softest silky underwear, presses the tummy that wants to burst like a bubble wrap, ready to pop under your eager fingertips. With an appropriate sound effect, of course.

While gaining a few pounds over the holidays can be a common reason for your tummy to inflate and uniform to shrink—not to mention after a heartbreak and a daily dose of big-box-of-ice-cream indulgence—there are many more causes why bloating happens. And bloating while flying is a special category, you'd agree. Let's not forget that whatever happens on the ground can only be amplified up there, in the air.

Being the badass *Skybabe* that you are, you must already be familiar with a few scientific facts about the impact air and cabin pressure have on us. At least from the knowledge gained from the very first training you had or you are about to have before officially spreading your wings in the sky. And although it might sound unnecessary to repeat, sometimes we brush it over our shoulder and completely pretend it is not happening to us.

Imagine, it is!

The pressure affects everybody, without exception.

You. Me. All of us. Period.

So, what is really going on up in the air?

Before we go into any further deets about health and travel, boo, we really just wanted to make sure we have your attention.

Are you ready for takeoff?

Then, let's go.

AWAKEN YOUR INNER BADASS

And suddenly, you just know it's time to start something new and trust the magic of new beginnings.
Unknown

2

Gettin' Outta Town

PACK YOUR BAGS, SKYBABE! WE'RE GOING PLACES

You can't cross a sea by merely staring into the
water.
Rabindranath Tagore

Peachy peach,

Many years ago, while taking my final exam at the university, I came to the realization that my ordinary life was no longer serving me. I was sick and tired of studying day and night and dreaming of the life I actually wanted to live. While sitting in a hundred-year-old amphitheater and eagerly finishing my exam, I finally admitted to myself that I would not play it safe anymore.

I was just about to graduate, and of course, look for a job I did *not* want. I had offers from several companies, but not one single offer made my heart flutter. I knew there was more out there. I felt it deep inside.

Just as I set my pencil down, I glanced at the clock and smiled. *This is done. Where to next?*

So, I began seeing in my mind's eye exactly what I wanted out of life. I visualized the job I desired. I imagined the place I wanted to live in, and I thought about how much I craved the change. I could no longer hide my disappointment from myself and the powerful urge to follow my dream of traveling the world.

I was 23, zealous and keen, nostalgic for the places I hadn't even seen yet.

I didn't know exactly how this was going to happen, or when and where I would go, but I knew I needed to take the first step and apply for the position.

I will never forget the day my mom came home from work and threw a local newspaper on the table in front of me. The full-page advertisement of a major international airline that was recruiting in my city stared at me. I had thought about becoming a flight attendant but never really looked seriously into it.

Wait. That's not true. Let me go back. *Way* back.

Third grade. I wanted to be a stewardess (this is what they used to call us back then). I wrote about it in my diary. I mentioned it in a school essay. And I even pretended to be one during playtime. Plus, my godmother was a flight attendant and I couldn't envy her more for flying around the world. I remember standing still for long moments of pure admiration while staring at her sky-blue fitted suit, high-heeled shoes, and white gloves. I indulged in her stories and rewrote them in my diary as if I were the one who experienced them.

Well, I also said I'd marry Schwarzenegger, but that's another story.

As a nine-year-old girl, I'd carry a small wheeled trolley through the passages and hallways of my building entrance whenever I'd go outside to play with friends. I also made paper money bills out of old brochures and magazines and made sure my pink velcro wallet was always full. Whenever I would see a kid or a friend on the street, I'd open my wallet and give them some money. Sure, they thought I was crazy, but it worked. This strong and very clear visualization helped me manifest the job I desired, and later on, with the job came the money.

Anyhoo, going back to the moment that changed my life.

While my classmates eagerly awaited the news of the next recruiter who would offer them a measly position, I was already on the plane to a faraway, promised land.

Was I happy? For sure. Was I scared? You betcha!

But while I had a dream of becoming a flight attendant since the third grade and saw myself flying from a very early age, I didn't know where the job would take me. I'd been traveling with my family since I was a little girl, so seeing new places and hopping on and off planes wasn't all that new to me. I'd visited many countries by the time I was eighteen, lived in a host family for a year to learn a foreign language, and spent two months in the city of my dreams that had been on my vision board since I was six. So, traveling itself never terrified me, but leaving my family behind for an indefinite period of time and venturing into the complete unknown seemed like something only the toughest would endure.

Of course, this didn't stop me and after three strenuous days of tests and interviews, I passed with flying colors. Even if I hadn't, I would have tried again and again and again. Because this dream lived in me for so long, it was waiting to come out.

Regardless of the difficulties, I stepped on that plane. I flew far away from home. I embraced the uncertainty. I shook, and I trembled. I cried through sleepless nights. But there was no way I was going back.

While my wobbly knees and sweaty palms told one story, my thudding heart and insatiable soul knew this was right. It felt right. I knew I'd made the right decision, and I knew it was one that would change my life for the better. For good. No matter how difficult it may have been, it was still something I needed to do. Something I longed for.

The very thing I manifested.

IS FEAR STOPPING YOU FROM PURSUING YOUR DREAMS?

Ah, here we are, *Skybabe*. You know exactly what I'm talking about.

I just told you about my biggest dream and how I worked toward achieving it. Yes, it took years of hard work and determination, but I knew I would make it. And while my path may have seemed easy and paved to success to onlookers, it was quite the opposite.

While I jumped for joy most of the time, there were moments where I wanted to hide under a rock and cry. I feared the big change that came with the job and the unknown future lurking around the corner. But I did it anyway.

Had I allowed fear and self-doubt to stop me from going after one of my greatest dreams in life, I wouldn't have had the joy of experiencing how I felt each time I set foot on new soil. I never would have known what it was like to swim with the sharks in the Seychelles, experience Mount Fuji in springtime, or get lost in the lush rainforests of West Africa. I never would have felt the excitement of learning new things and coming to know different cultures up front. Or visiting a local community and donating all the money I had on me for a school development program. These moments make life wonderful. They validate our purpose and show how much we can do.

So, to experience life, *Skybabe*, get out, and explore the world.

That's right. Look, if you ever let fear stop you from doing something your heart and soul so ardently wanted you to pursue, I hear you. But I also want you to know that those fears are all in your mind. They are made-up stories we tell ourselves. And they exist in our heads only. Danger is very real, and that's a fact. Of course you are going to think twice when crossing the street. But it's up to you to choose whether the thing you fear is real or imagined.

Everything I experienced in life until now helped me to grow. Good and bad. Even now, when I venture into something new, I still get scared. I let my mind serve shitty stories on a silver platter daily. But you know what I do? I do it anyway. It may take some gentle nudging and serious butt kicking, but I still do it.

Do you see where I'm going with this, *Skybabe*?

Mistakes will happen. Lousy people will try to make you feel bad. You will fail. But who the heck cares? You and only you. In other words, fear holds you back from living the life you were created to live and the life you inherently desire. That bullshit story you keep telling yourself why you cannot do something isn't real. It's just your fear keeping you stuck in one place because you think you don't have what it takes to move forward and do it.

When I got a job offer to fly as a flight attendant, I was slightly terrified. Yes, my heart leaped for joy when I got the news, but as the excitement settled and I began to prepare for the journey ahead, my gut clenched with dread. I had no idea what was waiting for me there and so many people told me I'd be back after a couple of weeks. That I was venturing into something too daring for a young woman.

But you know what I said?

Screw 'em! I went for it anyway.

Of course, this was a stepping stone to all my dreams I had planned for myself since I was a little girl. Yes, a stepping stone.

By accepting the challenge and getting out of my stinky comfort zone, I stepped into a magnificent future. And just like pearls on an extravagant *Cartier* necklace, my dreams kept stringing along the path one after the other—because I took the leap and allowed myself to experience it all.

IT'S JUST YOUR IMAGINATION PLAYING TRICKS ON YOU

It probably is, *Skybabe*.

But don't worry. There is a solution.

Instead of being scared and spending time to worry, why not do some visualization?

Allow me to explain.

When I was fourteen years old, I went to see a neurologist because of my frequent sleepwalking episodes.

I know what you're thinking, boo—she must have a screw loose. But I promise you, I'm not crazy. I even have a certificate to prove it.

At the time, my doctor did extensive testing that included EEG, Rorschach's Inkblot Test, EQ and IQ Tests as well as The Myers-Briggs Type Indicator Assessment, and after careful observations concluded that I was an extremely visual introvert with a vivid imagination, which wasn't that usual for a typical teenager. This was when I noticed that living in a colorful world and putting colors to feelings, seasons, countries, numbers, and even my dreams had a major impact on how I lived and perceived my life.

One night during this time, I had a vivid dream that I saw the famous Sydney Opera House from my room. The dream was so realistic that my dad found me by the balcony doors, staring out the window in the middle of the night. Australia had always been pink in my mind and ten years later I was in Australia, watching the magnificent New Year's Eve fireworks. The sky that night was bright pink. Just as I had always imagined it.

So, since then, after I realized that everything I had ever manifested through visualization was closely connected to the colors I saw it in, I started giving colors to each day. And if you're like me, you can start doing the same.

Now, *Skybabe*, here's a simple exercise that will help you distinguish real from imagined (fear). This helped me realize that for years I lived in denial, telling myself that I knew exactly what was worth pursuing and what wasn't.

It's easier than you think.

I want you to open your Skybabe Journal and write on top of the page:

Things I'm afraid of:

(Think of anything, even the tiniest bugs you might find frightening because I do understand these fears can be very real).

On the next page, write:

Things I'm afraid to do:

Give yourself a moment to think of all the things you are afraid to do. I am not talking about bungee jumping or climbing Mount Everest, but the things that are within your reach, things you think about daily but are afraid to do. For example, asking someone out on a date, asking for a raise, leaving the dead-end job you despise, getting out of a toxic relationship, moving to a new country.

So, let's try.

I want to ...., but I tell myself that I ....

I want to ask Jason on a date, but I tell myself that I am not good enough for him.

Now ask yourself what it is that you are imagining that is stopping you from going further: I'm imagining being unworthy of love. I'm imagining him saying no and I hate to be embarrassed.

Think about it. Has this actually happened to you before? Maybe. And that's why you have these reservations and envision the worst, especially if you already went through a similar experience in the past. Now, go back to that moment and play it out as if it worked out perfectly. Even if the person you wanted to ask out is no longer an area of interest, just show yourself that it's something *you* CAN change.

Thinking does not overcome fear. Action does.

Sometimes what you're most afraid of doing is the very thing that will set you free. Putting yourself out there is scary and thinking that you cannot do something because it seems hard will only get you stuck in the same place you've been for years.

Trust yourself, *Skybabe*. Change is a continual process that doesn't happen overnight. Remember that it takes time to build a better, stronger version of yourself, so enjoy every minute. Let it become a part of who you are. Think about all the risks you are willing to take and write them down.

Then, as the brilliant author Susan Jeffers says, "Feel the fear and do it anyway."

3

Believe You Deserve It and the Universe Will Serve It

MANIFESTING YOUR DREAMS

I dream. Sometimes I think that's the only right thing
to do.
Haruki Murakami

Skybabe-san,

Do you believe in dreams? Are you afraid of how big they are? Or maybe you're not sure what you want. Don't worry. We've all been there. I invite you to take a deep breath and look inside of you. Close your eyes, put your hands on your heart and listen. Listen to the answers your heart is giving you. Listen to your gut. Listen to the sound of the intuition you innately have in you. What does it say?

Discover what you want. Ask for it. Believe. Receive it.

The Universe has your back, *Skybabe*. Always.

·♥·♥·♥·♥·♥·

Sitting in the tiny Japanese language classroom, I listened to my high school teacher explain the new lesson and some weird-looking *Kanji* (one of three Japanese writing systems) we hadn't studied yet. I loved my Japanese teacher and her contagious enthusiasm. It was my first year of exploring this beautifully challenging, unique language and having a teacher like her was so motivating that it made me believe I could conquer the language and one day speak it fluently.

I would often picture this faraway land, the country of the rising Sun, its people, sushi, origami, kimonos, sumo wrestlers, bonsai trees, Zen gardens, and manga comics. But above all, cherry blossom trees in springtime. Her Majesty—the magnificent *sakura*.

It was late April and all the trees in my city were already in full bloom, including the two *sakura* trees in front of the school entrance. Those two trees, together with one more in our city's Botanical Garden, were the only specimen of Japanese cherry trees in the entire country. Now, if you have never seen this flower in full bloom, you don't know what I'm talking about and might think I'm crazy, but the beauty of it simply surpasses any other I've seen in nature. And one of those two trees in front of the school building was facing the window of my classroom.

During classes, I'd often gaze outside, indulging in the gorgeous views of cherry blossoms. In my mind, I would drift away and travel to Kyoto, Japan. Besides having been the old Japanese capital, Kyoto is famous for its beautiful temples and parks, brimming with magnificent *sakura* trees during the flower-viewing season.

Nevertheless, all my travels happened only in my imagination, because my reality was very different at the time. I barely had any money to buy a snack during school lunch breaks, let alone plan trips and travel places.

And that's all I ever wanted to do.

Travel.

And I knew I eventually would.

How?

I didn't have a clue.

The future didn't look so promising, but I kept believing in my dreams with inexplicable certainty. And until then, I decided I would read as much as I could while transporting myself to different places through books and images. I would imagine them the way I wanted, creating all those colorful worlds that existed in my mind before even stepping outside of my country.

The first thing I decided to do was to do volunteer work in the school library. This way, I was surrounded by as many books as I could imagine, since I couldn't afford to buy any of them. Oh, how I loved the smell of old books, and the cracking sound they made whenever I'd open them. I loved spending time in the library. Only now, when I remember and think about those high school days, I realize that those were the exact experiences that helped me develop my creativity and imagination. And the pure desire to believe in my dreams.

Just as Henry Ford once said, "Whether you think you can, or you think you can't, you're right."

So, what did I do? I decided to think I CAN and believed in it with unwavering faith.

Skybabe, I always used to say: "I know I'll travel the world. I know I'll live abroad. I don't know how, when, or where, but I know for sure I WILL."

The funny thing is that for me, in my mind, heart and soul, *it was already done.* It already happened, and I was certain my future would somehow become what I wanted it to be.

I will travel places. I will see the world. I'll spread my wings and soar high.

Still, to this day, I don't know how I started getting those high-vibrational ideas, but I know I did. And the best part? They worked!

Some took more time to manifest, some happened almost instantly. Some are still waiting for their right moment to realize and flourish, but it sure is remarkable what our subconscious mind can do for us when we work on it.

After four years of intense studying and exploring the Japanese language and culture, my life took a turn in a completely different direction. As it headed more to the West, I started focusing on other languages and experiences. But, the desire to visit Japan during *hanami (*cherry blossom season) was something I used to call my "lifetime wish" and kept it on my official Bucket List.

Fast forward a few years and several giant steps later, I found myself in *Skybabe* uniform. The girl who barely had anything but her dreams. The one who covered the walls of her room with colorful calendar photos of all those gorgeous destinations she dreamed of visiting. From white sandy beaches of tropical islands of Bora Bora and the Maldives, to the magnificent temples of Japan and mountain Fuji covered with snow. I believe that looking at them every single day, in the room where I spent most of my childhood and adolescent years, had a major impact on me.

These splendid images stayed deeply engraved in my subconscious mind.

Funnily enough, when I became *Skybabe* I thought that getting to Japan would be a piece of cake. And then, *wham!* I was hit with the reality of working as a flight attendant.

And the beauty of flight scheduling.

Here's what I mean.

After months of waiting, I finally got my first-ever flight to Japan. The dream that had been brewing inside my mind and heart was finally coming to fruition and just hours before departure, I was *the one* taken off the flight. Does this sound familiar, *Skybabe*?

"Operational reasons. We're sorry for the inconvenience."

"WHAT? You're sorry? No! No! No! You don't understand! I am not just a regular girl who's happy and excited to go to this beautiful country. NOOOO! I've been waiting for this my ENTIRE life! Do you hear me?"

I couldn't accept their answer. Nope! I struggled and stayed on the phone for more than half an hour with the scheduling officer, who was the one to inform me about it. There was no way I'd give up, and while he didn't want to be rude and hang up—which he could have done while leaving me disappointed and in tears—he simply wasn't able to help me. I'm pretty sure he thought that there was a great mix of craziness, inexplicable persistence, and remarkable passion in the girl on the other side of the line, something he didn't see every day. I honestly didn't care, but whatever he heard from my side made him put in extra effort to secure me another flight to Japan in two weeks' time.

THE POWER OF PERSISTENCE

It was almost winter that cold, gloomy November. There would be no *sakura*, of course. Still, I was ecstatic, for I would experience a late fall in Japan. And the moment I stepped onto this magnificent land, I sure felt like I was on another planet and not just an island far away from home. Everything was majestically different and deliciously new.

Since that first taste of Japan, I visited the country many times, but my manifestation, my high school dream and vision, would come to life after almost 9 YEARS of flying!

When I finally found myself in Kyoto, surrounded by dainty pink petals, everything made perfect sense. I'd waited for so long for this moment and because of that, I appreciated the heck out of it. Just as mesmerized and delighted as hundreds of Japanese around me, I gazed at the magnificent *sakura* in awe. As this glorious moment unfolded in front of my blissful eyes, I knew I had tapped into a well that would never dry out.

But let me tell you, *Skybabe*. Even that flight in March didn't come easy. It came with a set of obstacles that could have easily made me turn my back on everything.

Here's the rub.

To view the *sakura* trees in Kyoto, the city I wanted to be in, I had to be on a flight to Osaka since Kyoto was just a short train ride away from Osaka. But, instead of Osaka, I got Tokyo on my roster. Now, Tokyo is about five hundred kilometers away from Kyoto. Are you following, *Skybabe*? I know it sounds confusing but bear with me. As crew members, we have to respect a set of strict rules when it comes to our whereabouts. There are limits to how far we can go while on layovers. But when you wait for more than two decades to get to the magnificent place you dreamed about since you were a kid, you're ready to break ALL the rules.

Luckily, Japan is a country where punctuality and technology work like a charm. So, I planned the whole trip on my own, without telling any of the crew where I was going. We reached the hotel after midnight, which gave me a few good hours of sleep before waking up at 6 a.m. to catch the fastest bullet train in the world at the time—the glorious *Shinkansen*.

Mind you, getting around Tokyo isn't easy. Even for the Japanese who live there. The city is simply huge and if you don't plan your steps properly, you can easily get lost. And for the girl who only had a few good layover hours to fulfill her glorious dream, each step had to be planned c-a-r-e-f-u-l-l-y.

So, once happily seated on the train, I tried to get some shuteye but simply couldn't get my mind to rest from all the excitement. Sure, I was heavily jet-lagged from my previous trip to Miami just three days prior to this adventure, but I was thrilled and overjoyed!

After about three hours, I got to Kyoto Central Train Station and eagerly hopped on the bus. All was fine until I realized I was headed for the wrong park.

What a perfect opportunity to practice my stale Japanese skills! I stopped two local girls to ask for directions since they were going to the same park to see *sakura,* just like me. I jumped on a different bus and finally got there. After over one thousand kilometers, four different trains, buses and endless walking paths, before returning to do my flight back home, I made it to Her Majesty. *My sakura* tree.

Can I get an amen, please?

It all felt surreal. So surreal that for the longest time, I couldn't believe it was all happening *for* me. Right in front of my very eyes. Like I was in a fairytale from one of my library books, or a teenage girl surrounded by not two, but hundreds of familiar trees.

I couldn't believe I had made it. If there was a happiness scale from 1 to 10, I was definitely an 11 or more.

I did it!

Immersed in scents and colors, I walked in silence, enjoying the sounds and peacefulness around me.

Thank you, Universe! My lifetime wish came true.

And the whole flight back home, I couldn't sit still. Even though I didn't have a moment of rest before the flight since I jumped into my hotel room just in time to answer my pre-flight wake up call, I flew through that tin can while most of the passengers slept and colleagues dragged their feet.

And this is, my dear *Skybabe*, what it feels like to jump up and down in pure delight when you see your dream come to life.

BELIEVE IN THE PROCESS AND DETACH YOURSELF FROM THE OUTCOME

Another big dream of mine has always been to jump on the clouds. Yes, you read that right. *On* the clouds. As if that's possible, right?

Be it for the Simpsons and the clouds in the opening scene of this famous animated sitcom, or just for my creative lucid kid's mind, I often had these pictures of me jumping from cloud to cloud in the perfectly blue sky. Bouncing from one to the other, I would cuddle, snuggle, and hug them, but I would never fall. Because I believed I was always safe.

That sense of freedom in the sky represented the feeling I longed for. As kids, my sister and I watched people jump out of small planes with parachutes. The excitement, the adrenalin. It all looked so liberating. Yes, the fear factor was there, but the desire to do it at some point in life prevailed. So, I threw reason out the window and booked my venture.

I remember landing in beautiful Sydney, Australia, all geared up for my skydiving plan. It was probably my first year of flying as *Skybabe* and I was eager to explore every single destination I was going to. And already at that time, there were rumors about how good, safe, and beautiful it is to do skydiving in Australia and New Zealand.

Now, although this is considered an extreme sport which you are definitely not supposed to do on a layover, I disregarded the rules, yet again, as many *Skybabes* previously did. My dreams were much more important and now that I was so close to fulfilling another one, I wasn't going to stop. It was *my* life, after all. And my signature on that paper proving that I took full responsibility in case anything happened to me during the fall. It sounds scary, doesn't it? Oh, even as I write this, I get all worked up that I want to do it again.

Early morning the next day, I found my way to the meeting spot the agency had sent me. Together with five other people, I climbed that small bus and soon we were on our way to the outskirts of Sydney. Eagerly, we got on that tiny plane—a minuscule flying machine with rice paper doors—without the safety I always felt when flying regularly for work.

I swallowed a hard lump in my throat and took a seat. The engines roared for takeoff and I squeezed my eyes shut as the plane climbed the sky.

What the hell am I doing here?

I didn't tell my parents or my sister or my best friend that I would be doing this today. Not to mention my company. Was I crazy? *Definitely.* But that's not important right now.

Panic suddenly engulfed me, but one glance at the instructor who stood by the door as cool as a cucumber gave me a shred of hope. Still, when it was my time to get up and approach the door, my knees turned to water.

Who made you do this, Nena? You! You're out of your mind and you're going to pay for this. Now get your shit together and jump!

Of course, the crazy one by the door was my partner. The one I'd be jumping out of the plane with. And just as he muttered, "Do not linger and do not hesitate once at the edge of the door. Just jump!" I froze.

Well, munchkin, that letting go of the door frame was the hardest thing I had to do up until that day. If you'd already done it, you know what I'm talking about. But if you've never tried it, know that I was already shitting my pants. Still, deep down, the tiny devil, my crazy alter ego, laughed and urged me to let go.

Besides two couples who came together and provided a much-needed support to one another, there was one more person behind me. I didn't know him, but funnily enough, he was a pilot. And as that precious moment sneaked up upon us, seconds before the inevitable jump, the captain behind me screamed at the top of his lungs: "I can't do this! I'm afraid of heights! I'm afraid of heights!"

His words smacked my already worried face. *What is he talking about? He's a freaking pilot!*

And then it dawned on me. He wasn't the only soul. I knew that hundreds of my colleagues had the fear of heights and still bravely put on their uniform to go to work every single day.

I briefly turned to the frightened pilot, who was now as pale as his bleached shirt. At that moment, something suddenly flipped in me and out of my mouth flew a few welcoming words of encouragement. He glanced at me and smiled. And then, off I went. Like the best student, I didn't hesitate. I threw myself out, surrounded by nothing but blue sky and soft, fluffy clouds. That liberating feeling I felt for so many years while I watched skydivers with my sister came true. I felt it again. Only this time, I had a full body experience.

Brave and proud of myself, I kept soaring through the sky.

After safely stepping with two feet on the ground and kissing Mommy Earth, I was contemplating another jump. It was that addictive! But knowing I wanted to do other things in Sydney, I left. Exhilarated yet calm. Exhilarated for the wonderful experience, and calm because I acquired the certainty that everything, without exception, will always find its way to me, if I only wanted it badly enough. One more dream fulfilled, one more tick off my Bucket Dream List.

Life is good. Thank you, my dear sweet Universe!

4

Now Would Be a Good Time to Be Anyone Else but Me

EMBRACING MY INTROVERTED SELF

> Knowing others is wisdom, knowing yourself is en-
> lightenment.
> *Lao Tzu*

I peeked my face through the heavy gray curtains, gulped, and took a step back. My heart rate kicked up a notch, and my breath froze. Who would have thought that something so simple would be so hard? That I'd have a moment of complete panic before I was about to accomplish what I was paid to do.

Even the muffled sound of the engines and the cries of unruly children in the back couldn't take my attention away. My mind was focused on one thing only—the gigantic crowd behind those heavy drapes. I wiped the sweat off my forehead, straightened down my tabard, and took a deep breath.

I can totally do this.

I slid the curtain open and swallowed a hard lump in my throat. As their eyes locked on my meal cart, I could feel the anticipation.

I could see their hunger. Four hundred famished souls devouring me with their hungry eyes.

My colleague who was serving from the other cart was behind me, waiting for me to enter the cabin. Her impatient sighs and occasional eye roll only added to my anxiety. With a deep sigh, I raised both arms, placed them onto the cart handle, and released the brakes.

I'm going in.

Armed with only a smile and a cart full of meal trays, I counted silently in my head and stopped at row ten. The passenger I addressed first did not expect to be served so fast. With zeal in his eyes, he smiled at me and waited for his meal like a puppy eagerly waiting for his treat.

This was the moment of truth. I placed the tray on his table and grinned. Then I moved to the next seat and so on. There was no going back. I had them in the palm of my hand.

I breathed off an easy laugh. This wasn't that hard after all.

Now, boo, you're probably thinking, you've got to be kidding me. This can't be the worst thing! You go into the cabin, scatter some trays around and that's it. So what?

Well, it definitely isn't that difficult. And it wasn't the worst thing I had to endure.

Was it horrifying?

Absolutely.

For an introvert like me ... wait, wait, let me say that again. For a hermit crab like me, who had always been terrified of crowded places, this was probably the hardest social thing I had to do up until that moment in my life.

As a quiet, tiny girl with giant pink glasses on her skinny face, who was labeled as weird and different and bullied throughout the early school years, I always stayed away from people who were mean to me. I loved shiny pink notebooks and enjoyed sniffing and reading old books. I was always happy when it rained because rain meant that people stayed indoors, and I was free to wander the streets alone. I loved reading romance novels and dreamed of finding my perfect guy who'd love me for who I am. I hated intense discussions and any kind of confrontation and violence. I still do. I avoided large gatherings, and I never attended parties of the people I wasn't close to. It was just the way I was and how I protected myself. A quirky part of me that nearly cost me my job during training.

That's right.

I was literally yelled at for being too quiet and too observant during my crew training days. Of course, I completed all the courses and passed the tests. But just because I wasn't as loud as the next Jenny Blabber didn't mean I wasn't good at my job and didn't know what I was doing. The fact that I was an introvert and an individual, didn't mean squat to my insensitive training instructor. Talk about cultural differences and personality profiles.

Let me paint a clearer picture, *Skybabe*. If you didn't know me and you saw me at a party where I thoroughly enjoyed myself, you'd think I was the biggest extrovert out there. But that's because I'm most probably surrounded by a group of people I know well. Not the crowd of hundreds of hungry eyes waiting to eat me alive.

See, pumpkin, introverts notice everything. Because we don't talk as much as our extroverted friends, we tend to see the world differently. We notice all the tiny details and pay careful attention to what is happening around us. And we can see through other people. Others may think that we are unaware of humans and situations around us, but what they don't know is that we have eyes in the back of our heads. We're not assholes. On the contrary. We are nice, loving people who can get pissed at others because we see right through their baloney. And while this is difficult to accept by many, it's the truth, which is why people often misunderstand us.

Furthermore, being an introvert means so much more than just shutting the door to the world and recharging your batteries. It has everything to do with how we deal with the world around us. And because we cherish and understand different cultures, traditions, and thinking—especially if they're different from our own—we're sensitive to other people's problems and circumstances.

I can't tell you how many times I had situations like this on board. I remember once, a passenger made a joke my colleague did not understand entirely, but I perfectly got his sense of humor. In truth, he was just being charming and polite, but his demeanor and the fact that he talked rather fast (what we introverts do when we get overly excited and want to impress others) didn't sit well with my colleague. So, naturally, she got upset. When I spoke to her afterwards, she was mad at me for not reprimanding the passenger for being insensitive to both of us. This was absolutely not the case, especially later on when I got to speak to him again and learn more. She let her lack of understanding influence her behavior, when, in fact, all she should have done was ask him to repeat the sentence.

And here, we come to one of our strongest strengths.

Adaptability.

I know for sure that I can literally mold myself depending on who I'm with. And if I can't figure someone out straight away, which rarely happens, I say little or nothing until I know who I'm supposed to be around. That's why when we are around different people, we act differently, and this has nothing to do with being fake. On the contrary, this is because we have different comfort zones around certain people (one of the strengths my manager at the time noticed about me and I wholeheartedly thank her for that). Between you and me, *Skybabe*, I think she was an introvert, too. She got me.

Here's another way to think about it. Have you ever felt during a discussion a great deal of heat inside your chest that wanted you to speak up because your integrity wouldn't leave you alone? Still, you knew, if you said anything, you'd regret it. Because, let's be honest, it always sounds better in your head than when you voice it out. The never-ending problem of *should I say it quickly* turns into *I'm gonna say it* until you say what you wanted and then hear your words echo in your head, especially when no one acknowledges what you just said. Soon the guilt of *I never should have said anything* haunts you and there you have a perfect recipe for sleepless nights and overthinking—my life for an infinite number of years.

But we don't like to talk when we don't have anything meaningful to say. Right? We're gentle, caring, and complex. Our rich inner life is rarely shared and understood by others and that's why people label us as weird. We find meaning in everything, from our relationships to events and ideas. And even when we know the truth and know what happened, we will choose to pretend we're clueless just so others don't bother us and make us explain.

Despite learning all this at different life stages, later on, I became an emotional eater (addicted to sugar), to help me deal with my struggles. I suffered in a toxic relationship with a narcissist who made me believe I was hard to love. I went out of my way to adapt and be that perfect girl in his eyes, but no matter how hard I tried, I could never be "normal like all other women" as he wanted me to be. I was too quiet, too smiley, too thankful, too skinny, too emotional, too caring, too weird for some people. And there was no way I could please everyone.

But back then, I didn't see it that way. I'd spend sleepless nights dwelling on a simple mistake that had no impact on my life, but I worried how others would perceive it. While pretending to be someone I was not, I became the most authentic people pleaser, paralyzed by perfectionism and fear of not being good enough.

The list goes on.

Crippled by the need to justify my actions and thoughts constantly, I became my own worst enemy. And all because I couldn't define who I was or what I wanted. Now, when I first learned that I was an introvert and what this actually meant, I thought there was something seriously wrong with me.

Have you ever felt this way, *Skybabe*? Even if you're not an introvert, have you ever doubted your inner guidance and that little girl in you who always knew the way, who's been strong and passionate about the things she kept herself away from because others told her she's not smart enough, pretty enough, or good enough?

For me, this feeling was more pronounced during big life changes where I had to encounter large groups of unknown fellow human beings: when I first started high school, a new job, or when I moved to a new country.

Tired of feeling overwhelmed all the time and letting others dictate how I perceived myself, I forced myself to sit down and write about everything that was bothering me. Everything that was wrong with my life. I started studying and analyzing my habits and actions to find out why I was unhappy and to understand what I was afraid of. Then I made a list of all my dreams that I had forgotten about for so long. I wrote down everything I ever wanted to do since I was a little girl. This process was a revelation to me because right then and there, I realized I was in charge of my life, and only by taking massive action I could make that change happen.

If you tend to question everything about your life and yourself because you don't know who you are, *Skybabe*, this exercise is perfect for you. Before you start, make sure you find a quiet place where you can answer the questions in peace. Take your beautiful journal out and write everything that comes to mind.

Ask yourself:

- **Who/What do I want to be?**

- **What do I want in life?**

- **How do I want to feel?**

This fantastic exercise helped me learn to love the truth, to be honest with myself first and then with others. About what I need, how I feel, and who I am.

No matter how harsh and unpleasant it may have seemed, once I wrote it down and became aware of it, the truth was the first thing that set me free. And all because I learned to filter information and focus on what matters. I refuse to give my time to negative people and thoughts. If something is poisoning my mind and soul, I simply won't give it a chance to enter my life.

This exercise helped me let go of the past. Sure, it was hard, but it's so wonderfully liberating not to be imprisoned by thoughts and actions that once made me feel so small.

Over time, I learned how to deal with loud, repetitive noises, unpleasant smells, people, crowds, and not being able to unwind at the end of the day (something difficult and, at times, impossible for us introverted *Skybabes*).

Now here's the most important part: **you are who *you* decide to be, *Skybabe*,** not what people think of you. When you accept yourself with all your flaws and imperfections, you understand that most of these negative thoughts came from other sources, not you. They came from your surroundings that you blindly followed and believed in.

Learning who you are and knowing your sensitivities and strengths will give you great confidence to do anything you want in life. Always remember that your past relationships and actions do not define you. **You don't need validation from anyone. You decide who you are, how you feel, and what you want.** And if someone tells you that you're weird, reserved or different, just thank them for their opinion and move on. **Their opinion has nothing to do with you and with who you are.** It has everything to do with how they see themselves. **Their inner battles are not your battles.** Their beliefs, thoughts and opinions are not yours to worry about.

Because *Skybabe*, know that you are an incredibly amazing and interesting person to be around. Someone who can talk about the

Universe and human existence on Earth, holistic health, evolution, psychology, philosophy, peace, compassion, and love. Someone who is in love with the natural world and can spend hours gazing at the stars and clouds. Someone who travels and sees the world through fresh eyes.

Now think about and answer the following questions:

* **How have you modeled yourself to fit the expectations of others?**

* **What were you taught to believe about yourself that is untrue?**

5

You Are the One Thing in Life You Can Control

LETTING GO OF CONTROL AND BEING OKAY WITH IT

> What worries you masters you.
> *Anonymous*

Ah, *Skybabe*,

I remember the day I overslept and missed my flight. My plane left at eight o'clock and I woke up at 08:05.

Imagine the agony!

The moment I looked at my clock and realized the alarm hadn't gone off, I panicked. Now, if you knew me personally, you'd know that I'm never late. I plan ahead of time and prepare in advance just in case unpredictable circumstances occur, so I am perfectly ready to handle them. But when something like this happens, my life turns into a living hell.

I immediately started calling crew scheduling to beg them to put me on any flight just so that I wouldn't be marked absent for the day. But here's where things got even more interesting – I spent the next six hours on the phone, only to get a busy signal or no reply at all. While still in my PJs! I wasn't going to get another flight as I had planned earlier, and there was no way around it.

Remembering the situation and what led to it, that same week, I had the flu that left me bedridden for days, with high fever, headache, and everything that goes with it. The night before, I went to bed early, hoping to catch some zzz before my flight. Since I hadn't slept well the previous five nights, I finally fell asleep peacefully and got the rest I needed. And while I woke up feeling energized and refreshed that morning, I realized I had missed my flight, which turned the whole situation around. I started hyperventilating and going utterly berserk over a situation I couldn't control.

The plane was gone.

I was late.

The world kept on spinning.

Still, if I had handled the situation differently, I would have never allowed the stress to overpower me. I could have just turned around and had some more sleep, or simply spent the day on the beach. But the more I focused on the stress, the more it agonized me. The truth is that control is one of the methods I used to stay safe and keep things in order, but what I forgot to notice that morning is that I cannot control everything in life.

What will my boss say? My friends and colleagues will think I'm negligent and irresponsible because I missed my flight.

These were just some of the thoughts that went through my blurry mind that day. The thoughts that kept me paralyzed for days to come. But the reality was that no one knew. And no one cared. Nobody suffered, flights went on as planned and everything fell into place.

I missed the flight that day, but every cloud has a silver lining, *Skybabe.* I also missed the biggest typhoon that hit Hong Kong and Taiwan that week. This meant that the airports were closed and even if I had made my flight that morning, I would have probably diverted to a different destination. Still, it took time to realize this. Things *do* happen for a reason, and sometimes all we have to do is accept and let go.

So, how do you respond to what you can't control, *Skybabe*?

Do you let the situation run you, or do you purposefully act, knowing how you want to feel and see it unfold?

First of all, **look at the big picture** and understand what it is that you can and cannot control. When you gain clarity of the situation, you'll get a better picture of why you worry so much and soon realize that worrying won't change anything. And more often than not, you'll see that these worries are minuscule and that *you* have power over them.

Next, **say no to drama.** If drama develops around you, take a step back. More importantly, stop playing the victim to circumstances you created. I thought I was having a problem that couldn't be solved, forcing myself to believe that the mess I put myself in was so big that I focused all my energy on it and created a scene that got out of control. **But how you choose to look at a problem will directly influence how you deal with it, *Skybabe*.**

So, if you decide to look for a hidden meaning within that problem, you can use it to grow and refuse to be defeated.

Focus on what you can control. The one thing you can control is YOU, so decide how you respond to what is happening around you.

Moreover, **be thankful.** Whatever happens, know that better things are coming. I believe that if I don't get what I think is right for me, something much better is on the way, which always proves to be true. I've learned that the more grateful I am for each experience in my life, the more goodness comes back to me.

Whenever you think a negative thought or start worrying about something in the future that most probably won't happen, you project it onto yourself. You bring it into your life for no reason. When a negative thought comes to you, and you are about to say it out loud, don't finish it. Reverse it. Use it to your advantage and say what it is that you truly want.

The Universe sends you exactly what you are ready for at the exact time you need it in your life. Stop acting small, thinking that you deserve only as much as you think you should have.

So, take full responsibility for your life and make it what you want it to be, *Skybabe*.

Stop making excuses and start making changes.

When you stop blaming others for your failures and circumstances and take full responsibility for your actions, you become unstoppable.

Now, it's time to take your journal out and answer the following:

- **What is one thing you find hard to let go, but you know you cannot control?**

Write down five things you're going to stop worrying about this year:

1.
2.
3.
4.
5.

L-O-V-E

Someday, somewhere — anywhere, unfailingly, you'll find yourself, and that, and only that, can be the happiest or bitterest hour of your life.
Pablo Neruda

6

Un Viaggio Chiamato Amore

A Journey Called Love

A kiss, and all was said.
Victor Hugo

Hey *bambina*,

How's your flight so far?
I know I'm gonna ooze that wistful sigh out of you and possibly make you cry a little, but bear with me. This is a happy story, so just sit back, relax, and enjoy.

It was late at night when I finally got the chance to lay my head on my pillow and get some well-deserved shuteye. Still, I wasn't in a hurry to fall asleep as I had only a few more hours on standby and I knew I'd be able to relax fully once the time was up. My mind was glued to the idea of having a relaxing day off the next day with plenty of free time to lounge by the pool with my newest bestselling read.

With all that in mind, I knew the scheduling couldn't call me for long layovers. Even a quick turnaround wouldn't ruin my mood because I knew I'd be back home in no time with the rest of the following day off. With a blissful smile, I exhaled a sigh of contentment and turned to the side, carefully going over my day in my head.

Ah, the joy of being on standby. And the delight of knowing that crew scheduling can screw you over in an instant when your phone rings just 45 minutes before your allotted time ends.

Grrr.

I growled and cursed as I got out of my warm bed, with the idea of having to be completely ready in full uniform and makeup in forty minutes.

As I got straight to the airport, I learned that the flight I was called for had been delayed and instead of going through the crew channel, I had to go directly down the terminal in order to reach the aircraft on time. And with all the crew and passengers already on board, I was the last one to show up.

Oh, glory! One more thing to be grateful for.

Imagine the faces of angry passengers when they saw me rushing inside the plane. In their minds, I was the reason we were delayed and then, out of pure zeal, with a voice of an angel, the cockpit crew announced that due to sudden changes in requirements, the company had to add one more crew on the flight.

And she was late.

Yep, that's me, in case you're wondering. *Thank you, Captain. Whoever the hell you are!*

I was the one who always huffed and puffed when someone boarded the plane late, even after ground personnel deployed an army of skillful hunters to search for lost Duty Free shoppers. But this time it was me. And I wasn't shopping. I was sweating to the point of exhaustion just to reach that gate on time. I was planning my day off. I had better things to do than to fly that early morning. Yep, yours truly was late, through no fault of her own.

So, I got in and literally, seconds later, the doors closed and we were on our way to ... *bella Roma*.

At least the destination was right.

Somewhere after the first meal service and a few fainting passengers (yes, you read that right), I went around the aircraft to say hello to my colleagues. Since I'd missed the briefing, I didn't have a chance to talk to any of them face to face. Naturally, to most of them, I was just a blurry image of a crew member in uniform, and might as well be as insignificant as the next passenger. But I was determined to meet everyone, and after all, it was my duty to do so.

Of course, my last stop before going back to the aft galley was the cockpit. Can't mess around with that. I had every intention of making myself known to the flight deck, just in case. Off the top of my head—hijacking, or God knows what. If the Captain had the power to decide who's who in a highjacking situation, I wanted to make sure he knew I was on his team.

But to be perfectly honest with you, chatting with the flight deck crew was never on the list of my favorite things to do. I never relished the idea of sitting in the jumpseat behind them, casually chatting about their dull lives. Rarely, there was an interesting skydiver or an adventurer who'd draw me in with his stories and make the flight more interesting. See, while I loved being in the cockpit, because—best view ever—I was never interested in small talk. So, with a deep breath and a huge smile on my face, I rang the door, smiled at the camera, and within seconds, I was in.

From the angle where I was standing, I said hello to the First Officer, who turned and welcomed me with a smile. Then I turned to the Captain and reached out my hand to greet him and properly introduce myself. "I was pulled out for this flight and never had a chance to say hi, so here I am ... yada yada yada ..." I continued with my gibberish until his gorgeous smile smacked me right in the middle of my rumbling belly.

"Hello, there."

And then my jaw dropped. Hearing the deep, somewhat eager voice, I lowered my eyes to a ruggedly handsome face with dark chestnut hair that perfectly matched his bright white teeth and tanned complexion. *Hello, Captain Handsome. I ... mean ... Hanson.*

At first, I was slightly embarrassed because it was obvious that he saw my immediate reaction, but how did I miss that cute smile of his?

Right. The standby.

After exchanging pleasantries and a few meaningful words (hint, hint), I learned that Captain Handsome had never been to Rome. Imagine a pilot with a rich career and tens of thousands of flying hours behind him who had never been to the Eternal City.

He was a virgin!

Hold your horses, boo. Not that kind of virgin. At least, that's what one could assume, with his handsome face and athletic physique. A layover virgin meant one thing and one thing only: I had to show him around one of my favorite cities and possibly find out more about his interesting flying life.

And of course, since I had visited Rome for the *nth* time, even in my short flying career, it was my obligation to show him the place. Only, there was one teeny tiny problem. *Screech!* The rest of the crew. Female crew, that is.

How do we get rid of them?

On my way out of the cockpit, I came up with a carefully crafted plan that would help me get my hands on that stud muffin. I sure wasn't the only one thinking this way. But there was something that clicked between us and I knew we were destined to do this flight together.

We reached the hotel and after collecting my allowance and room key from the reception, I zoomed by a group of colleagues and dashed inside the elevator. With one hand firmly pressing the third-floor button and the other tirelessly hitting the 'close door' switch, I waited for the doors to slam shut before releasing a major sigh of relief. (Any fellow introverts out there? I hear ya!) When I was in the clear, walking toward my room, I snatched the room list from my pocket and glanced at the names. My eyes immediately darted to the top of the page and my Captain Handsome was in room 515.

And then the realness of the moment hit me like a Mack truck on a cold, drizzly day. I knew he wanted me to take him to Rome, but we never made any plans.

As you read this book, *Skybabe*, you already know that I'm pretty shy around new people. Shy, timid, reserved, introverted, hesitant, nervous … weird. Whatever you wanna call it. But flying has taught me one thing: when it comes to important matters, especially when they involve handsome-as-hell pilots, who cares what others think. Shy or not shy, you gotta do what you gotta do. Still, there was no way I'd pick up the phone and call him. I'd rather jump off a cliff than experience that trembling heartbeat and sweaty palms. Plus, I didn't know anything about the guy. He could have been married and the last thing I wanted to do was meddle in his affairs.

So, I left it to fate.

I got ready and decided to pay my favorite city another visit. I had plans on where to eat, what to see, and what to buy. And to my big surprise, the elevator doors opened and my Captain Handsome's radiant smile welcomed me in. And not just his, but the smiles of three more female crew members, fake as one-inch nails on a delicate feminine hand wrapped around his elbow. Talk about going from a high vibe to a subzero state of mind in an instant.

Nevertheless, I kept my cool, said hello to everyone, and stayed quiet for the short ride to the reception.

Upon exiting the hotel, he was there to open the door for me. When I climbed up the stairs to the bus and sat by the window, he sat right next to me and smiled. "I thought you weren't coming."

My heart thudded in my chest and my cheeks went hot. *Deep breaths, lassie. You're right where you wanted to be.*

Exactly. We were sitting next to each other on our way to the Eternal City. Struggling to contain a grin, I turned to him and said, "I told you I'd take you around, I just wasn't sure *you* were coming."

Anyhoo, we talked, we laughed and the time it took us to get to the city center went by so fast. With a big smile on my face, I got off the bus and informed my colleagues that I was on my way to see my aunt, who was eagerly expecting me.

Now, let me be clear with you, *Skybabe*. There are still some things you don't know about me. Some flight attendants have lovers in every port of the world. Some make new friends wherever they go. I, on the other hand, had an aunt in all corners of the globe. Yes, even in the savannas and woodlands of Africa. Not joking.

The truth is that I never liked going out with the crew on layovers. This was especially true if I was going to a new destination. The last thing I wanted to do in a brand-new place was justify myself to a colleague I didn't even know that well. If you know me and you were on one of my flights, no hard feelings. It's nothing personal.

It was always the destination and me. No one else.

First, yes, I was shy, and I found it hard to share my free time with a bunch of people with whom I had already spent the whole working day. Second, I wanted to explore the new place myself. I wanted to indulge in the scenery and fall in love with my favorite parts. I wasn't sharing my time with anyone. This is not to say that I never went out with the crew. I did. Occasionally and usually when I felt like it. Most of the time, it was great. But if I didn't feel like it, I'd just tell them that my aunt was waiting. Sometimes right at the bottom of the Spanish Steps, oftentimes at a café along the Seine, or right in the middle of the Brooklyn Bridge (which actually isn't that far from the truth).

So, soon, Captain Handsome and I were on our way to my beloved imaginary *zia's* house.

I wanted ice cream, Captain Handsome wanted pizza. We agreed to separate briefly even though my layover virgin stuck to me tightly for orientation and safety, only to meet again at one of the timeless meeting points, *Piazza Navona*.

Enwrapped in conversation, we headed toward *Via del Corso*, witnessing the most famous sights in Rome: The Colosseum, the Roman Forum, and further down, *Piazza di Spagna*. After tossing some coins in *Fontana di Trevi*, we had a few more scoops of *gelato* at a corner *gelateria*, watching the locals run out and about as the day unfolded in front of us. And then, we stumbled across a few marvelous places without even looking for them: a tiny bookshop that sold flowers and served espresso, a miniature shoe seller that had the most colorful shoe display in the window, and *Roseto Comunale* for a tranquil retreat with the most beautiful display of roses and breathtaking city views.

We had a good few hours to cram all the Roman gems into our precious layover time, that we even made it to the Vatican. As we eagerly waited to get inside the famous St. Peter's Basilica, the guard at the door shot me an unwelcoming look as his thick eyebrows drew into an angry frown. *"Scusi signorina, così vestita, no!"* he said, pointing his finger at a giant sign by the door.

Of all days, I had to wear a sleeveless shirt that day. Rookie mistake!

But wait, I wasn't a rookie. I'd done this numerous times. What was I thinking? Well, Captain Handsome and his charm may have had something to do with it. Nonetheless, he was the one who offered me his sweatshirt by covering my shoulders while sending a smug smile in gate guard's direction.

Take that, gatekeeper. I'm going in!

With plenty of time to spare, we visited the Vatican Museum and, of course, Michelangelo's masterwork, *Capella Sistina*.

One thing I reminded myself that day, apart from making a mental note to always have a pashmina shawl in my purse, was that Rome wasn't about the shiniest, fanciest monuments everyone was raving about. Sure, they were fascinating, but the hidden details we encountered along the way made all the difference. The tiny things tourists don't see. But after countless visits to the Eternal City, it becomes more like home. Or a book you loved so much you read it four times. A timeless movie or TV show you just couldn't stop watching.

My heart jumped for joy after one of the best layovers I'd ever had. Not because there was a gorgeous guy in it, but because it was filled with thoughts, emotions, and deep, meaningful conversations.

There was only one thing that got in the way.

I knew it wouldn't last.

My very handsome Captain Hanson told me he accepted a job in another airline, in a faraway city, on a different continent, and was leaving in two months' time. I heard him and nodded when he said it, but my heart and mind disregarded it completely. Still, I knew nothing serious could grow out of our relationship if we ever chose to have one. So, I embraced the moment that was offered and enjoyed it. We spent a wonderful day in Rome, had an amazing flight back, and finally, we said goodbye. I was happy I took the chance and went out with him. Something I never would have done if I hadn't felt that spark when we said our first hello in the cockpit.

And the more I think about that day, the more I realize we were two people destined to cross each other's paths. That day helped me mend a broken heart from a previous relationship and move on. My serendipitous meeting with Captain Handsome was like a breath of fresh air. A revelation and a moment of pure joy embedded in my mind, reminding me that if I wanted to make a change, I could.

Anytime in life.

And by accepting to go out with him, I accelerated my healing process. My fairytale was short-lived and had to come to an end, but I knew it was for the best.

So, *Skybabe,* if you're wondering if it is possible to have a relationship while flying, here's what I know for sure: finding romance while flying isn't hard. But finding a lasting, meaningful relationship is.

Now, I know you're probably thinking, "But you meet so many people, you see so many wonderful places. How is it possible that you never bump into anyone significant?"

Oh, you do. You run into different people and cross paths with strangers you'd never even dream of meeting. Like that crazy-rich First Class passenger who says he'll buy you three houses and a luxury car if you marry him. No, not *him.* I mean a breathtakingly handsome doctor in green scrubs who tells you that you're beautiful as you cross the street near Columbia University after attending a free writing class (talk about #thingstodoonalayover). Or a glance from a sexy stranger in the London Underground that leads to an hour-long intellectual conversation on your way to the city center.

These are just some of the sparks that happen as you trot the globe. Yes, some people will leave you wondering and some will leave you breathless. But the reality is that while flying, sometimes all you want to do is crash for the night, drool on your pillow, and start afresh the next day. Or go out and explore the city on your own. Sometimes all you want to do is fall in love with a new place. It's a feeling similar to falling in love with spring, or a new puppy. It makes you fulfilled and in love with your life, which brings a completely different meaning to it.

Even when I craved a solid, steady relationship, I still chose to find joy and peace in the little things that made this job completely worthwhile: a stroll along Tokyo's Ueno Park, a zesty gelato on Ponte Sisto over the Tiber river, a show on Broadway. Of course, seeing all these amazing places would have been much different if there had been someone special to see them with, but it was all worth it. And the more I think about it, the more I realize that the solitude made all the difference. It made me get to know myself better and learn to appreciate my time alone.

And when it comes to dating and relationships, everyone's story is different. If I had a penny for every time someone asked me why I didn't have a boyfriend *yet,* I'd be jumping up and down with glee, counting golden coins in my vault.

Yes, I admit, I longed to be in a relationship, but more than that, I yearned for a deep and meaningful connection. And most of the time, this was hard to find because of the nature of the job, but it doesn't mean it's impossible. And I know many *Skybabes* who thrive in their marriages and partnerships. Somehow it's even sweeter because you get to miss that special someone even more when you're away and every time you meet again, it's like a mini new *rendezvous.*

That day in Rome brought new beginnings for me and opened my eyes for something I denied for too long – love and acceptance of myself. When my eyes landed on that handsome pilot's face, all I wanted to do was to learn more about him and spend as much time on our layover together with hopes that our chance encounter would turn into something significant and long-lasting. Sure, I spent countless days daydreaming about falling in love with him. Not to mention that every time I thought of him flying that beast of an airplane, my nerves would flutter.

He was sexy and powerful, and he made me laugh.

But while my love affair didn't unfold according to my immediate expectations, that day turned out to be a day to remember. A day that culminated in a heart-stopping kissing scene in a forgotten corner of the city where few tourists venture. Somewhere among the centuries-old ruins and lush green gardens, there we were, sharing a kiss that made being in Rome that much sweeter.

So, my dear, sweet *Skybabe,* I want you to find that love. Whether in a museum in Paris, a corner *gelateria* in Florence, a Michelin star tofu restaurant in Osaka, or a secret farmer's market in Kampala, I want you to experience it.

Wherever it may be, promise me you'll enjoy it.

7

En Cada Puerto Un Amor

LOVE IN EVERY PORT . . . NOT REALLY

Some love stories aren't epic novels, some are short
stories. But, that doesn't make them any less filled
with love.
Carrie Bradshaw

THE VATICAN MADE US DO IT

It was wintertime. Big, fat jacket time. Boots, gloves and mittens time. Hot tea time. Good old classic book time. Romantic Christmas movie time. Definitely *not* sightseeing time.

But there I was, seated in my jumpseat, all excited and eager to land and still go out. Tapping my toes against the floor, looking through the small window of my designated door while extending my neck like an ostrich, I gazed at the outlines of the beautiful Eternal City of Rome.

It was my birthday. Yes, it was *that* time of the year.

The streets and *piazzas* decorated for Christmas. Or for me? I'd always wanted to believe it was all for me. A bit of egocentrism is allowed on your birthday, isn't it?

The wheels touched the ground, and before long, we were gliding down the runway toward our gate. *Good landing, Captain!*

And as soon as the warm, welcoming Purser's voice streamed through the passenger announcement system, I knew we were there. Eager to get out of my seat, I waited for the seatbelt sign to switch off. And then, that pleasant voice came back on again, only this time, it was a special surprise announcement about my *compleanno*. Big applause followed the joyous words and soon I found myself receiving numerous *Tanti Auguri* from the elderly ladies and gentlemen coming from Australia with whom I had been chatting throughout the flight. There were many couples who couldn't speak English well, so we bonded easily because of my Italian. It was a moment to remember, and soon after, we came to a complete stop.

I was so happy to be exactly where I wanted to be on my birthday—in Rome. In one of my top three favorite cities in the world and surely in my favorite country. Italy, you are *semplicemente bellissima, la più bella del mondo!*

Ciao, ciao a tutti! Grazie! Arrivederci! Ci vediamo!

And soon enough, disembarkation was over. We were free to go. After doing a quick lost-and-found check together with my colleagues, I hastily collected my stuff to get off the aircraft. Hopping on my dancing feet like Pippi Longstocking in between seats (don't ask us how we manage to pass so skillfully through such a narrow space, but you know we do), I got the looks and smiles from the cleaners already coming on board. A happy-go-lucky crew member with a giant grin on her face? Not a usual sight!

For the busy Fiumicino Airport, we passed the immigration point surprisingly quickly and were soon on the shuttle bus to the hotel.

Eccoci!

We were finally there!

The wind blasted and although I just needed to cross a tiny pathway from the bus to the entrance door of the hotel, my hat fell off. I jumped to catch it, then carefully placed it on my head. Dragging my suitcase and cabin bag through the ever-so-annoying revolving door, I headed straight toward the reception. *I'm here, ready to celebrate MY day! Bring it on!*

But, wait! Something caught my eye in my peripheral vision. Someone whose face I knew well was sitting on the sofa to my right.

My head whipped around so fast I heard it crack. It *really* was him. And he came all the way to Rome to see me. Really?

See, *Skybabe,* two months ago, seeing him would have made my heart leap in my chest from all the excitement. But right at that moment, I was petrified. A tendril of panic started to creep up my arms and into my chest. I held my breath and for a moment I felt like all the air was trapped in my lungs and I couldn't breathe.

Why is he here?

All of a sudden, I forgot I was in Rome and everyone around me quickly faded into blurry figures. My joyful, ecstatic expression suddenly turned into a frown, and I dropped the suitcase and turned. I wasn't sure if I was happy or sad, excited or disappointed, but I knew I was still heartbroken. And yes, he was the one who shattered my heart in pieces.

I had no idea what an appropriate reaction would be, but I knew at some point I'd have to face him. As I inched my way to him with my eyes glued to his, he stood up and leaned forward, as if expecting me to kiss him, but I didn't. I couldn't. I just looked up and gave him a courteous smile. And then, a barrage of questions overran my already clouded mind. *Where is he going to sleep? Should I let him stay in my room?*

I didn't want to see him again after what he'd done to me, but a part of me was nudging me to give him another chance. After all, he came all the way to Rome just to see me. The least I could do was let him stay in my room.

The bed situation? We'd figure that one out later.

Silent and slightly agitated that he'd messed up my birthday plans, I walked down the corridor toward my room with him behind me. He trudged his way forward, quiet and calm, as if waiting to see my reaction now that we were away from the rest of the crew. I knew deep down I still loved him, but I was *not* ready to forgive him.

As we entered the room, I put my suitcase and cabin bag to the side, without allowing him to help me. I took off my jacket and threw it over the armchair. This was probably the only time my uniform didn't end up on the floor in less than two seconds and without my lipstick smeared all over his face. Whenever we'd meet while we were together, he was hungry for me. Hungry for my kisses, my face, my body. The passion we shared only grew stronger with years and distance. Nothing ever changed there. Living in two different countries, the distance and the time only increased the longing and expanded the desire to rip that uniform off and make love immediately. He was never the guy who waited. And he never asked for permission. I felt overpowered by his sensual desire, and I loved it.

But this time, it was different. He was patient and somewhat insecure, staring at me with the eyes of a sinner, waiting for his wrongdoings to be forgiven.

I felt his longing. I knew he wanted my warmth, my heart, the loving look in my eyes. But I couldn't say a word. I sighed. And then I cried. A river of tears. Unstoppable and inconsolable tears that shook my body and made my mind shrivel.

His immediate reaction was to step forward and take me into his strong arms. I felt like Charlotte Brontë's Jane Eyre in the arms of Mr. Rochester. Fragile in his tight hug, lost on his chest, eager to stay there forever but also yearning to leave and never go back.

It was a romantic movie moment. Heavy but tender. Familiar. Whatever I thought I had achieved until then, while healing my broken heart, just disappeared. It dispersed all around in a thousand pieces. I was confused and shattered, but I was still in his arms.

We didn't speak much. After a while, we got ready to leave for the city center. I decided I didn't want to waste a second longer and was adamant about seeing Rome on my birthday. With or without him.

I purposefully deleted all the details of our day in Rome because it would have been too painful for my soul. What I chose to remember were some amazingly beautiful moments we shared while we were together. Moments filled with love, pain, and magic. His eyes meeting mine as we held each other in a tight hug in front of *Basilica di San Pietro* in the Vatican. A lot of apologies, promises, and moments we'd missed. And I fell for it. Because I still loved him.

My intuition never gave me a sound yes, but I went for it. And because I never had that clear sign deep down, I knew we wouldn't last. While our relationship continued for several years after that day, it was filled with suffering and anguish throughout. It wasn't love like I knew it before. We dragged us and our relationship for years, having the highest of highs and the lowest of lows.

He just wouldn't change. And who was I to try to change him, anyway?

But after everything I'd been through and the love experiences I'd had, I must say that his effort to keep me was what made me stay. You know, *Skybabe*, he was that guy who was never lazy to do anything for me. With him, everything was figureoutable. He would drive for half a day, sit on that plane, jump on a train, and just come see me, to spend less than 24 hours of my layover with me. He would always find a way, even though I never asked. Maybe I didn't see it then and maybe I never admitted it to him, but that was *huge*. And to me, it shows commitment which is rare to find nowadays. And just for the record, up until today, I never found out how he knew my schedule, my flights, and hotel information. He was a proper Hercule Poirot when he wanted to be, including that one time when he called my hotel room number in Tanzania. Wow, talk about creative ways to tell someone you love them!

As a couple, we couldn't move forward anymore and as much as we tried to mend our relationship, after many years, I decided to let it go.

ARE YOU A STUDENT? NO, I'M A PROFESSOR!

"Gabriel, wait! Are you crazy? What are you going to tell him?" I yelled after my dear French colleague as he strutted into the cabin to talk to a First Class passenger.

My Passenger.

The One.

Now, pumpkin, let me explain. Although I met so many men on board and would often get an endless number of business cards we all are familiar with, I was rarely attracted to any of them. There was no way I'd make a move, dial the number, and get in touch with the person on the card. Not saying it didn't happen. It did, but for me, it was once in a blue moon kind of situation. Most of the cards would end up in the bin, either in the aircraft lavatory, trash-compactor, or while clearing my pockets at home. While most of those guys were surely annoying to me, some of my friends found lifelong partners on board. But my story is somewhat different.

Gabriel came back to the galley, all smiling and radiant, with a mischievous grin on his face. "He likes you. And he wants to talk to you more, but says you're shy. I told him you are shy, indeed, but that you like him, too, and that he needs to make a move."

Oh my goodness! Is this for real? How will I ever enter the cabin now and work until the end of the flight?

"This is not happening, Gabriel! No, please, tell me it isn't!"

My cheeks burned. Oh, how I wished I could retract my turtle head and disappear until the end of the flight, pretending I was just a random seat handle or some piece of equipment or whateverrrr.

But facing my cute tall African man *again,* talking to him, looking at him *now* after all this, I was lost. Lost for words, or any kind of action. I tried to avoid the side where he was seated, running around like a puppy chasing its tail. And to add to my misery, Gabriel secretly communicated with him behind my back.

It was almost the end of the flight and there was really no way for me to skip going into the cabin. I had pre-landing duties to complete right where my gorgeous gentleman was seated. There was no other way but to face him.

And a woman's gotta do what a woman's gotta do! Capeesh, munchkin?

I went back into the cabin, and as audacious as he was, he waved his hand to ask me a question. His beautiful face stopped me in my tracks as his eyes studied mine. I honestly hoped my cheeks didn't look as red as they felt. Hearing Gabriel's giggles behind me, I stiffened as my embarrassment steadily turned to humiliation. Bless my friend for he was only trying to help, since I secretly admitted to him there was someone I really liked but didn't know what to do. So, as any good friend would, he took the situation into his own hands.

But most importantly, I wanted to do this for myself. I wanted to meet this stunning gentleman, ready to allow myself an adventure I'd always dreamed of. Sentence after sentence, our pleasantries soon turned into quite an engaging conversation, as much as the time allowed us to do so. I could see that with each comment I'd made, he was getting more and more curious to know not only about me, but how my brain worked. He noticed the sharpness in my answers, the specific details I would gladly and effortlessly provide to any of the questions he posed like a nerdy college grad. Then, all of a sudden, he asked, "Are you a student?"

I pulled in a deep breath and smiled. "No, I am a professor!"

I truly was, and in my country I held a title of a language professor. Apart from all the teaching degrees I had at the time, I was and am a teacher for life.

His pupils widened, and his radiant smile burst into sweet laughter. I felt there was something in me he wasn't able to resist. He suddenly seemed even more interested, asking endless questions to which I had answers, of course, but my pre-landing duties couldn't wait, so I had to leave him.

Holy guacamole! I was so proud of myself, *Skybabe*!

Trembling from excitement and embarrassed, with scarlet red cheeks, I felt his eyes on me the whole time, even though now I walked through the cabin with confidence, mirroring his huge grin.

As I sat in my jumpseat, I silently rewound the events of the day in my head, going through some important life dilemmas. Somewhere between A.L.E.R.T., N.I.T.S., and other safety procedures, I secretly indulged in the thoughts of my cute passenger. Because that jumpseat—the "electric chair" as I used to call it—indeed, is quite a peculiar place. The place where I had the most extraordinary thoughts—both positive and negative. I hardly ever imagined crash landing or any catastrophe in it, but rather the moments from my life flashing inside my head, reminding me where I was and where I wanted to be. I wonder if you or any other *Skybabe* had the same experience. I've never asked anyone so far, but I'm curious to find out.

But hey, let's go back to the tall, handsome man I was telling you about.

The passengers started disembarking, together with mine. As he passed in front of me, he stretched out his arm and slid a piece of paper into my hand. Too self-conscious to look at it straight away, I acted as if nothing had happened, but Gabriel, who stood right next to me, nudged me to do it. I glanced ahead of me and saw that my passenger was the last one to leave the First Class cabin, so I opened my palm and saw his boarding pass.

Oh, well. Okay. But then I had a better look and saw unexpectedly beautiful handwriting with a note and a phone number below it. He offered to take me out to dinner.

Excitement ran through me and although I wasn't really sure what I would do this time, I was happy that our encounter happened just the way it did.

I gave myself the entire morning and afternoon to rest, think and decide, but I knew if I wanted to see him, I had to act fast. He was just passing through my city and already the next day, he would be gone.

Finally, I sent him a message, and we connected. I could feel the eagerness in his replies. And from that moment onward, it was always exciting with us. We talked about everything. From health and lifestyle, to politics, music, literature, history, religion, culture, and the joy of life. We exchanged meaningful ideas and asked for each other's opinion. We were eager to hear what the other one had to say, comment, and add. I know he loved my wits, as I loved his. The jokes we exchanged were smart, sharp and bright, so that's why we easily connected from the very beginning. And funnily enough, it was quite impossible to argue or fight with him. I don't remember a single time he would even want to raise his voice or get into proving who was right and who was wrong.

I remember the night we had our first dinner together. Romantic dimmed lights, soft music playing in the background, an intimate atmosphere on the rooftop of my favorite hotel building with barely anyone around us. Although, I have no idea what we ate or talked about. Blank. All I remember are his eyes and a genuine smile on his stunning face. He was the perfect gentleman. Kind and polite, playing to my own rhythm. I couldn't really say much about his intentions, as he was so relaxed about everything, but as I was getting ready to leave, he invited me to his room.

Instantly, I drew back. I was sure he noticed the expression on my face, but soon told me he just needed to get something from his room before walking me down to the lobby. But that was enough for me. I had already built a wall, thinking about the usual stereotype of flight attendants and their love life. And I didn't see myself as one, no matter how much I liked him. I was grateful for the dinner, but I decided nothing would continue from that moment on with this guy. Not a chance!

And to my surprise, he really did get what he needed from his room and soon I was on my way home.

So, as life often unfolds in the directions we don't expect, our story evolved, too. My darling Assane kept on staying in touch, always being perfectly nice and balanced.

And patient.

And persistent.

He would never cross that line of respectful behavior, but after some time, he revealed that he wanted more. He wanted a kiss, at least. *No.* I was stubborn. Stubborn all the way. Not even a kiss. Nope.

Of course, over time, I started to miss him. When we were apart, we'd send each other emails on unusual topics. Although they had barely any love words in them, for me they meant so much more, on another, more profound level. Our discussions were witty and cute, and so was our communication in general. Nothing seemed difficult for him and it wouldn't take him much to arrange the dates, his meetings, schedules and get the ticket to travel on a flight I was operating to the city in Africa he used to live at the time.

Now, Assane was my passenger again, and this was some time after my flight with Gabriel. Even though we got to know each other better over time, we were hungry for more. Especially *him.* The flight kept me busy, but the entire time I knew he was observing me from his seat. And this time, I wasn't nervous. On the contrary, with him by my side, I felt secure and protected. His presence radiated safety, which was one of the traits that attracted me most to him. I was professional, and he was kind, as always. And the flight went by smoothly. Almost magically.

With a few loving looks from both sides.

One question kept repeating in my head over and over again. *What should I do with this six-foot-six guy and his disarming smile?*

He was a successful, highly educated, wealthy young man on his way to greatness. I had no problem imagining him as president of his country, as we often mentioned in our jokes. He was powerful and smart. A natural leader, he could talk to the prime minister or a taxi driver with the same ease. I truly believed he had what it takes, and I knew a brilliant future was ahead of him. Because of the social circles he was in, he would invite me to meet some of the politicians he was friends with.

This was when I realized how different our worlds were. The experiences I had with him made me think how I needed to up my game and go back to myself, to my studying, and personal and professional growth—all of which I had neglected since I'd started flying. I didn't allow myself to dive deeper into the relationship, because I couldn't see a future with him. And his constant presence in my life didn't make it any easier for me to make a decision and stick with it. But he was adorable and I couldn't resist his wits and charm. Even when he wore his red velvet shoes.

Time went on, we kept in touch. And he stayed patient. But when he got tired of tapping in place, he took the lead.

During one of my layovers, I was in his house after the flight and we had just finished eating a lovely dinner. After he showed me around the city, took me to his office, a famous historical site and a museum, he brought me home. This time I didn't refuse. I followed his plans. I could feel his longing for me. Mind you, we hadn't even kissed yet, so it must have been hard to endure the desire that had been piling up from within him.

There we were, at the dining table with our bellies full, looking at each other in silence. So, when he suddenly stood up to lift me from my seat and take me in his arms, I didn't say a word. He climbed the stairs and carried me to his bedroom, where he threw me onto the bed with great passion. And ... the rest is history.

Like everything else with him, it was smooth. It was wild. It was beautiful.

And while I didn't see how we might make our relationship work long distance, we still kept seeing each other.

Missing him was hard. Being away for long periods of time, even harder.

Months went by and one summer day, he asked me to come on a trip with him. He wanted to take me to a place I'd never been on a vacation.

Just him and me. He was just waiting for my *yes* and he would do the rest, as he assured me. He wanted us to have a good time and didn't want me to worry about anything. For a bit, I contemplated what to do, but then I accepted his invitation, which led to having one of the most magical romantic getaways I'd ever had in my life.

As you know, boo, since childhood, I've had colorful posters on the walls of my room. They were photos taken from the calendars with the most gorgeous places in the world and one of them was Cinque Terre in Italy in all its wonderful rainbow colors.

So, Cinque Terre, here we come!

We agreed to meet at Milano Centrale Train Station. I was excited to see him, but I wasn't sure what to expect. Yes, we had a relationship, but we weren't really a couple. Still, we did all the things couples do. I couldn't see a clear future with him, but we got along so well and when we were together, I didn't want the moments to end.

While waiting to meet him amid a busy terminal, the "over-thinker" in me didn't allow me to relax until my eyes finally landed on his. That was when my other side prevailed. The one that said,

Go! Enjoy this holiday with him! Chill! You'll have an incredible time! You deserve it! So, I allowed myself to feel, act, behave, and express whatever naturally came to me.

Surrounded by nature, we spent the next few days in a beautiful boutique villa up in the hills. We hiked along the trails from one village to another and took short rides on the train. We enjoyed romantic meals, tasting the homemade wine from the same vineyards we passed through. We kissed. We laughed. We made love.

To make the entire experience even more surreal, we continued our trip to Milano, where we stayed in a highly luxurious hotel in the heart of the city. I remember entering our rooftop suite directly from the elevator and a huge Jacuzzi which had our names on it. As cherry on top, in no time, he arranged for us to see Verdi's *Attila* in the famous *La Scala* Opera House, since that was something I'd always wanted to do.

I was head over heels for this man who took amazing care of me and showed nothing but love and understanding. But somehow, I knew our adventure was over. I allowed myself to feel and open up with all my vulnerability and emotions while getting more and more attached to him. The distance and time soon interfered in our love plans and we wouldn't exist anymore. My sixth sense was telling me so. And it was right.

This was his way of saying *adieu*.

With deep hugs and gentle kisses, we said our goodbyes at the airport and went our ways.

MY WILD DOLPHIN ESCAPADE

Islands have always fascinated me. Brilliant sunsets that light up the sky, turquoise blue waters, abundance of fresh exotic fruit, and white powdery sand between my toes.

Since the first time I visited an island in Greece, I knew I would forever be a devoted admirer of the islanders and their laid-back way of life. Hardly ever will you see an islander scurry down the street, overly stressed and in a rush. Even if they're late, which most of the time they are, they stroll and wander, completely relaxed. And as much as this trait sometimes (well, honestly, many times) went on my nerves, I also secretly admired it.

Maybe because I'm the exact opposite.

If you're like me, *Skybabe,* you've probably spent hours day-dreaming, wondering what it would be like to live on a tropical island. There's something special and calming about the sound of the ocean lapping at the shoreline while you lie on the beach. But when you find yourself soaking up the sun in some of the most majestic places in the world, you realize that dreams *do* come true.

And the islands were always at the top of my dream destination list. From Puerto Rico, Cuba, Jamaica, Aruba, and Curaçao to the Greek islands, Seychelles, Mauritius, Manado, Bali, Thailand, Zanzibar, and the Maldives, you name it! I've seen and reveled in their beauty with my eyes, mind, and heart.

Along with the wish to see and enjoy as many islands as I could, I had the desire to swim with the dolphins. I know this will come as no surprise and that many *Skybabes* wish to do the same, but for me this was a Dream with a capital D. I wanted to swim with the dolphins in the open sea. Wild dolphins, of course. Not in the pool! Never!

And this is how I met my own Dolphin. My Aquaman.

I sat on the edge of the speedboat with goggles, mask and fins on, eagerly waiting for the skipper's instructions to jump in and swim with the dolphins. We had already seen a bunch of them playing, saluting us with their friendly clicks and whistles, while some of them spun in the air. Ready and eager, I waited and waited until I jumped in. But it was *too* late. They were too fast. Still, I was determined to see them up close. So, I climbed up the boat in silence, happy I was close enough, ready to dive in again. People next to me screamed in excitement, telling their stories to one another while I patiently waited for my turn.

"When I tell you to jump, you jump straight away! Just follow me and do what I do. Okay?" I heard the voice of a man who was in charge of our tour. At first I didn't realize he was talking to me, but there was no time to think.

He yelled again, "Now! Jump!"

And so I did.

I was right above a cute family pod with a tiny baby dolphin. They were so close, but swam extremely fast, so they zoomed by us in no time. I had to speed up if I wanted to see more of them. Turning left then right in the water, I soon realized I had lost direction. To my surprise, the same man who told me to jump seconds earlier appeared out of nowhere. He looked at me with his smiley eyes, took my hand in his and led the way underwater to catch another view of my gorgeous dolphin friends. I watched as his powerful muscled body moved with effortless grace, as if he were part of the underwater world. The way he swam—how his body moved in the water—he truly was an amphibian. He held my hand and, without words, I understood I had to be fast and obedient, mimicking whatever he did if I wanted to see them again.

And then, the dolphins came back below us, mere inches away from my side. As you can imagine, this glorious moment lasted just a few seconds, but it left me mesmerized.

Dolphins don't wait for you to give them a closer look or take a selfie with them. They go on with their lives to play, eat, and even sleep with half of their brain awake while still swimming.

Insanely short in reality, to me, this moment was everything. Time stopped. It made me realize how incredibly grateful I was for the unmatched maritime wilderness I'd never witnessed until that moment. For this handsome man beside me and my hand in his. For the exceptionally clear, turquoise water and strong protruding sun rays all around us. For this magical, romantic bit of time that brought peace into my life, much like the surrounding silence.

"Wow! WOW, WOW, WOW! I finally saw them!" I screamed out with joy, giggling and splashing the water around me. Aquaman said nothing, just smiled.

"I'm so happy! You have no idea!" I babbled in excitement. "This has been my dream for years and you made it possible! I feel so happy I could kiss you!" I said and gave a gurgle of laughter. "Can I?"

He looked at me with a wide grin on his face.

Without waiting for his answer or permission, I swam to him and placed a soft kiss on his cheek. I did it without much thinking, to my own surprise. I *had* to do it. And it seemed he didn't mind at all and actually liked it as he gave me his warmest smile, confirming my kiss was approved.

And this is how it all started, boo. From our hands joined underwater, swimming in silence, to exchanging the feelings of utter happiness and excitement every time we swam with the dolphins. I fell in love with the story.

And contrary to what Ariel from *The Little Mermaid* desired, I slowly got to discover a whole new world ... underwater.

That day was the beginning of my island love life chapter. I'm not sure how I managed it all, *Skybabe*, as it wasn't always easy, but I kept going back to that isle and to him—my Aquaman. On days off, vacations, and layovers.

My amphibian man and I had many more magical moments together in the water with the dolphins. We'd wake up at dawn, have yummy vanilla tea and set out on the ocean, on his boat. I learned that dolphins play, sleep, and eat at different times of the day. I understood how not to scare them away by swimming in silence with my arms glued to the sides of my body. I learned to respect them, their habitat, and their intimacy. As Aquaman once told me, "You wouldn't want someone watching you sleep in your bedroom and constantly poking and waking you up, would you? We are just silent observers. That's all."

The more time passed, the more I understood the meaning of his words. And more than anything, what he was truly like. We as humans don't belong there and if we want to become part of the oceanic underwater world, *we* need to adapt, not the fish and the mammals.

I started seeing the environment with fresh eyes, especially when I learned that Aquaman was actively involved in environmental protection and other subject issues. I went on marine expeditions with him, which almost felt like I was part of the National Geographic Expedition Team. We saw humpback whales and bottlenose and spinner dolphins who welcomed us every time we set out on a new adventure. I adored riding on the bow, with sun and wind in my face, as the boat sliced through the waves. Before meeting Aquaman, I was afraid of swimming in the open sea, or even just being on a boat. But with him, all of my fears slowly dissipated. I trusted him more than myself and surrendered to that endless feeling of freedom only the ocean can give.

Spending time with him was a sort of therapy for me. I was officially hooked on island chillness, the bluest of skies, and living in the now.

In short, my life on the island was the perfect counterbalance to my crazy life in the sky.

8

Broken Girls Blossom into Warriors

Skybabe's Happily Ever After

Your scars are not your shame. They are your stories.
Atticus

Skybabe,

How do you tell a girl whose heart has been torn to shreds that she'll find love again? That not all men are the same and that the pattern she created for attracting losers into her life had deep, irreparable wounds she never thought she would be able to heal.

Mentally and physically abused, I thought I'd never manage to put the pieces back together for someone to love me the way I wanted. I learned to believe that love was hard to find, and that I wasn't worthy of it.

I'll never forget that night in Paris when I learned what love is *not*. Lights on Champs-Élysées, shoppers leisurely strolling down the busy avenue. And one pretty heavy punch in the stomach I did not deserve.

The night I confronted him on the balcony of a famous city hotel when I heard him say over the phone that he would be home in two days. The words that gave me the creeps and made my blood boil.

He. Was. Married.

Overwhelmed with the feelings of betrayal and helplessness, I pleaded with him to tell me what was happening. Anger raged in me as I demanded, and instead of an explanation, I got a big fat slap on the cheek. And then another one. And when he couldn't smack my face anymore, he kicked me in the stomach, after which I crumpled to the floor and prayed for my life.

I couldn't breathe. The initial shock of what was happening left me breathless and after the air escaped from my lungs, I found it even more difficult to breathe.

I needed to scream. I wanted to hurt him. My heart was urging me to fight, but my brain told me to keep calm in order to live.

So, I stayed quiet.

Silent tears streamed down my cheeks as his vague words and faint promises blurred my clouded mind. As moments passed and his anger dissipated, I came back to my senses, but I knew I had to get out of there.

Trying to avoid him for as long as I could, I stepped outside onto the balcony. Through a teary gaze, I stared at the Parisian landmark twinkling in the nearby distance, feeling resentment and sorrow. All I wanted was to fly back home, scrub the touch of his hands off my face, and crawl into the comfort of my bed.

It took many months to replay what had happened in Paris and learn why I allowed a creepy narcissist to treat me like that. I was a mature and responsible adult who came from a loving family and always cared for others. What was wrong with me? And why did I deserve this?

My fairytale ended, tumbling down, and I fell into the abyss with it. Only, it took time to realize it wasn't a fairytale at all. It was a delusion.

I was in love with a fantasy—an idealization of who I wanted him to be while turning a blind eye to the truth of who he essentially was.

The bruises on my body healed within weeks, but my wounded heart and reeling mind kept me restless. For the longest time, I hated Paris. Not because it didn't meet my expectations, but for the experiences I had with the wrong person while I was there.

I wanted romance. Long walks along the Seine while holding hands. A stroll around the cobblestone streets of Montmartre where Monet and Renoir found their inspiration. Instead, I lived through a nightmare no woman should ever have to go through.

Deep down, I knew real love was effortless. Not in a way that you don't have to work for it, but in a way that all anxiety, worry and bullshit disappear when you're with the right one. And I know this because I felt it. I lived it and I'm still living it now.

After months of recovery and healing sessions, I finally moved on with my life. I swore my fidelity to bettering myself and got clear on what I wanted out of a relationship.

And just like that, when I least expected it, he showed up. A confident, caring, handsome man. The one I thought would never want a broken girl like me. The one who showed me, before we even met in person, how a woman should be treated.

One email led to another and soon we found ourselves chatting daily in different time zones. He wanted to meet straight away, but I somehow delayed our date because I unconsciously tried to protect myself. I was safe behind my words, but I wasn't ready for a disappointment. I wasn't ready to learn that he wasn't the one. I wanted things to stay as they were, rosy and magical.

So, one early winter morning, I arrived in New York City. I didn't tell him I was flying in so early because I wanted time to rest before we met. Surprisingly enough, the hotel I was planning to stay at mixed up my booking dates, and I was left without a room for most of the day. Of course, you can never be bored in New York, so I visited the public library and a few of my favorite places before I went to meet him in front of the fountain in Bryant Park.

The park was busy as usual, even on a freezing winter day.

A brief thought slipped through my mind that we might miss each other in the crowd, so with intentions of changing our meeting place, I phoned him.

From a payphone on the corner of 42nd and 6th.

And just before I hung up, he was right behind me, greeting me with a smile.

Years later, we're still head over heels for each other. And no, things aren't always rosy and carefree, but we make it work. We go through storms together and find ways to make our love grow. And we sure as hell protect the magic we created.

We continued to travel and explore the world, and one day, we visited Paris. The city that had a whole new flavor to it this time. We kissed, we hugged, and we made love as the city bathed in shimmering lights in front of us. It was the city of love I wanted to be in. With *my* man.

I know you were hurt, too, and maybe you're still hurting, *Skybabe*. You want the pain to go away, but you just don't know how to deal with it.

I hear you and I feel you.

But here's the truth.

You're a fighter and you won't settle until you find what you deserve. The relationships I had in my past shaped me and taught me priceless lessons: to always trust my gut and never undermine my worth.

Today you might be stuck on the page you don't want to turn. I know how hard it is to turn that page, but your body and mind need you to move on. You must close the chapter that destroyed you and maybe even burn the book. Then open up a fresh page and start writing the way you want it to be.

You can't correct your past, but you can create a magnificent future.

No matter how hard you're hurting right now, know that you'll get through this. Forgive yourself. Forgive others who hurt you in the past. Then keep going. You owe it to yourself.

Healing from trauma takes time, but it's possible and it is something you have to do for *you*.

One step at a time.

And one day when you realize what it took to dig yourself out of that dark hole they once buried you in, you'll never want to go back to what broke you. Because one day, the Darkness will only be a distant memory and the Light will be your *now*.

Rejection is protection because something greater is on its way to you. Your soulmate, ideal partner, that swoon-worthy real-life romance novel hero or whatever you want to call him exists. And you will find him. Just know what kind of person you're looking for. Write it down. Feel the feelings of how you want them to make you feel. Live it daily and give it time. You're both on the right path, moving toward each other.

And when the time comes, you *will* meet.

9

The Big Deep Hole

Letting Go of a Toxic Relationship

You've got a new story to write. And it looks nothing
like your past.
Unknown

Note: *While we wanted to keep this book happy, witty, and adventurous
with the best intentions, we decided to include this chapter for any
Skybabe who may be stuck in a toxic relationship right now. We hope
you find it helpful.*

· ♥ · ♥ · ♥ · ♥ · ♥ ·

Baby boo,

You want to feel needed, wanted, and loved. You crave that
special someone's touch, kiss and affection, hoping that they'll love
you back as much as you do. And that's perfectly natural. But what
happens when you're in a wrong relationship, when everything you
do is to please your partner?

As a loyal, kind, and selfless person who constantly finds ways to make the relationship work, you give yourself fully. Your warm heart and beautiful soul, staying quiet just to please them.

You lose yourself. Your identity, dreams, and everything that you are.

And while you may think you're happy, deep down you know that the longer you stay with the toxic partner, the smaller and less confident you become.

The more they lie, manipulate, and criticize you, the more power they have over you. But the moment you put your foot down and challenge them, they become even worse. They start doing everything they can to put you back into that small space they made you believe you belong. Where you feel helpless and unworthy.

Remember, *Skybabe*, **toxic people are never changed by your kindness.** *Never.* They simply don't care. Staying invisible and quiet and giving yourself more to them won't help. It will only make you feel resentful, frustrated, and angry with yourself.

If it hurts you, makes you cry and question yourself and your worth, know that it's harmful and that you should leave.

Walking away and letting go means creating room for a better, happier, and calmer you. No matter how hard it may seem initially, nothing beats the feeling of freedom later on when you realize what you went through.

So where and how do you find the courage to leave?

Here are a few powerful ways that helped me break out of a toxic relationship. And while these steps led to many sleepless nights and heartbroken cries, in the end, they set me free.

I encourage you wholeheartedly to take a good look at your life and start making a change. You will see life from a completely new perspective, and just knowing that you are in charge of your freedom will make you unstoppable.

Keep a Diary

See your life the way it actually is. Write what you see and feel. Express your emotions. Vent, curse, cry, whatever you need to do, just make sure you write it down. Include all the little details of how the toxic partner makes you feel.

What feelings do they bring out in you?

Find What Makes You Happy

Finding the core of true happiness is difficult after losing your sparkle and being drained by the toxic environment. But there is a way to bring it back. Try going back to your childhood. Even if you find painful memories, try to think of all the things you enjoyed doing as a little girl. Hug a friend or a loved one, go outside for a long walk, draw, make art with your hands, take photos. Make a routine for yourself and know for sure that each day you are going to do one thing that will make you happy. Don't let anyone interfere with your plan, no matter how silly it may seem.

Know You Are Worthy

Remember that *no* is a full sentence. You don't have to explain or justify yourself for leaving and wanting to live a life you deserve. This may be the hardest part of leaving a toxic partner, but you need to know your worth. Tell yourself how incredible you are and believe in yourself so strongly that you'll want to stay away from people who don't appreciate you.

Spend Time Alone

Even though it may seem natural to talk to others in times like these, when you're hurting and all you want is a listening ear, it is important to spend time alone, too. Friends and family may want to help and give advice, but that doesn't mean that you have to take it. Spending time alone to sit with your thoughts and emotions can be excruciatingly hard, but necessary. And the right amount of solitude can be a wonderful thing when you're working on yourself. Also remember that breaking out of a toxic relationship takes time and energy, so keeping yourself physically active while nourishing your body can make the healing process more bearable.

Choose Happiness

Surround yourself with people who inspire you and bring out the best in you. If you can't find them in your surroundings, join online communities, read blogs, and listen to podcasts. Stay away from people who threaten your joy and try to drag you down. Invest in your personal growth: join a support group, hire a life coach or take a self-confidence course, or any course you feel called to do.

No one may hold you prisoner of any kind. Your health, safety, and emotional stability should never be compromised. You are a beautiful, unique, and caring person who deserves love and affection from the person who loves you for who you are and not for who they think you should be.

You are you, *Skybabe*.
You are unique and extraordinary. May you be more and more YOU every day.
You deserve to be happy.
Trust your intuition. You don't have to justify your feelings to anyone. Just trust your own inner guidance. It never lies.

Now imagine giving yourself openly to someone who cares for you and loves you just the way you are. Who puts as much energy as you into your relationship and appreciates all the little things you do to make life beautiful.

Love is nurturing, kind, and accepting. It makes you feel alive. It helps you grow. You deserve to be loved. You're worth fighting for, *Skybabe*.

Now take a moment to think about and answer the following questions. They hold power and we recommend you let everything out in your journal without censoring yourself. Then read your answers and reflect.

- **When you start a new relationship, what is the first thing you think about when it comes to the two of you together?**

- **Do you idealize your partner and wish they understood you in different ways? How?**

- **When a relationship is not going well, and you can't voice yourself, do you stay, or do you find a way to leave? Why?**

- **What makes you put yourself down just to keep your partner in your life when you know they are not right for you?**

- **Have you ever been abused or physically hurt in a relationship? What happened?**

- **What helped you heal?**

- **Do you often think of your partner cheating on you? Why is that?**

- **When your partner wants to be with you, but you have different plans, do you immediately change everything to accommodate their needs? Why? What will you do to change it?**

- **Does your partner give you a choice, or do they always decide how things will be? How often do you say what you want?**

- Do you know what you want in life right now, and why you are in a relationship with this person?

- When your partner mistreats you, do you state what's on your mind and become aware of your feelings, or do you stay quiet? Why?

- Remember the last time you said YES when your heart said NO. What happened? What was your heart telling you?

- Do you make time for your hobbies and interests, or do you give priority to your partner without thinking about yourself first?

- When you think of leaving the toxic relationship, what makes you stay? What do you keep telling yourself, and why?

- When was the last time you took time for yourself after your relationship ended?

- Describe what you do when you jump into a new relationship after a breakup while still holding onto resentment from the previous one?

- What do you think your partner can give you that you cannot give yourself?

Today you are you! That is truer than true! There is
no one alive who is you-er than you!
Dr. Seuss

ALWAYS remember:

Never apologize to others for their misunderstanding of who you are.

Stay away from people who make you feel like you are hard to love.

Don't make yourself smaller to make someone feel better.

You don't need validation from anyone else to feel good about yourself.

Don't let someone change who you are to become what they need.

Don't ever stray away from who you are to get closer to someone else.

Never run back to what broke you.

10

The Power of a Hug

A CHANCE ENCOUNTER

> So many people come into our lives and then leave
> the way they came. But there are those precious few
> who touch our hearts so deeply, we will never be the
> same.
> *Mary Englebreit*

Chiquita,

Do you believe in hugs?

I remember passing through Tokyo's Narita Airport several years ago and seeing a "hug station" where ground personnel offered hugs to anyone who needed them. Passengers with aerophobia (extreme fear of flying), families finding it hard to say goodbye to their loved ones, and anyone in between could get a much-needed embrace. It was a brilliant way to make someone feel better INSTANTLY.

And yes, **I believe in hugs.** And I know that they have magical, healing powers. I've learned this many times in life, and not a day goes by that I don't hug someone I love.

When I first started flying, I didn't see things the same way.

Young and restless, traveling the world but unsure of where I was going, I never took a moment to just sit and observe the world around me. I was in a hurry to see as many places as I could, thinking that this would always be easily accessible to me and that I will be young forever.

One late summer day, no matter how fast I was going, trying to escape life, I had to stop and face it. Because of bad weather, I got stuck in Seattle, having to wait for the next available flight home.

But my problems didn't end there. Because I was traveling on a standby ticket, I had to wait after all the passengers had gotten seats to see if there were any seats left for me. A tiny, sweet lady, Mary, who was on my flight, had the same problem. She was in her mid-seventies and needed to get to the UK as soon as possible. We started talking, trying to cheer each other up and find humor in a seemingly hopeless situation.

After hours of waiting and figuring out a plan that would get me on a flight back home, I finally learned that all the passengers would be given a hotel room and would fly out the next morning, since the flights were canceled for the day.

Of course, I did not get a room.

Mary didn't get one either.

We were both airline staff, and we had to deal with the obvious.

So, she asked me if I wanted to share a hotel room to split the cost. I agreed, and we continued our conversation. I didn't mind sharing a room with an elderly lady who reminded me a bit of my grandmother. Being there with her calmed me down, and all the talking and laughing made the time go by fast.

We were both exhausted, and she offered me to take a shower first. Now, remember that we could not get our luggage as it was stored somewhere at the airport, so all I had was my carry on that had a toothbrush, a shawl, and a notebook. No clean clothes or PJs to wear. Still, I was grateful for the hot shower and a place to sleep overnight that wasn't a cramped airport seat.

Once I got in bed and wished Mary goodnight, she continued with her regular bedtime routine. It was a process, as she called it. A few years ago, after an invasive bladder surgery, she had to wear an external urinary pouch. So, changing took time and taking a shower wasn't easy. But she was calm and neat and took time to get ready for bed, just as if she were at home. Then she took her medication, brushed her hair, and switched off the lights.

I was still awake and anxious, not knowing what tomorrow would bring. Would I get on that flight? Would they load my bag? Would I make it home on time to report for my flight duty? Then Mary asked if I were awake. I was trying hard to fall asleep, so I didn't say a word. But she kept going.

"Why do you worry so much? You are young and beautiful, my dear," she said. "Things will work out. They always do. We'll get on that flight tomorrow. You'll get home; I will reach London in no time," she continued.

"I remember when I was your age. It was almost half a century ago, but I can see it clearly as if it were yesterday. I am still that young girl inside. I am still me. Cancer made me realize I won't always be here. For years, I thought I had time, that life would be here forever and that I could just postpone it until the next day to finish other more essential things. I worried about the things that never happened and talked myself out of many wonderful situations I only dreamed of.

I was afraid to take risks. But soon I realized I was only postponing life.

I was fearful because I wanted to be comfortable and safe. And now, nothing to me is more important than life right this very minute. **To live each moment as it is.** Even in this stressful and hopeless situation, I found happiness and laughter. I found *you*.

I know I don't have much time left, but I still want to believe that my life was worth living. I lost the love of my life many years ago. I chose not to get married and have children. I chose to live alone. Time goes by so fast. Keep life simple and enjoy the smallest pleasures. **Don't wait for tomorrow. It's never guaranteed."**

The next morning, Mary managed to get on an earlier flight, and I waited for the afternoon one. Her words echoed in my head and would stay with me for many years to come. As she approached me to give me the good news, I stood up and gave her a hug—the one that told countless stories. The much-wanted, incredibly healing hug we both needed. Long and firm, calm and nurturing. The hug that turned into medicine.

Our stories came together in that perfect moment we thought we had lost forever. She got a bit of fresh air that lightened up her life, and I learned an important lesson that life doesn't wait.

That day, I found out that Mary was going back home to say her goodbyes. We didn't exchange numbers, but I wanted to call her and ask how she was doing. I wanted to tell her that things would work out and that meeting her helped me look at life from a different perspective.

Now, back to you, *Skybabe*:

- **Try to remember a situation where you didn't see a way out, but you made it through.**

- **What is truly important to you in life but you keep putting off?**

- **What would you say to your younger self with the life experience you have today?**

- **What is one thing you would regret if you didn't do it in the next ten years?**

11

A Grateful Heart Is a Magnet for Miracles

SKYBABE'S ATTITUDE OF GRATITUDE

When you focus on the good, the good gets better.
Abraham Hicks

Hey honey boo,

Sometimes it's easy to forget how wonderful life can be. We live on an abundant, incredibly giving planet that has absolutely everything we'll ever need. But when you're unhappy, unsatisfied, and unfulfilled, it's easy to overlook all the surrounding goodness.

Today, we'd like you to do a simple gratitude exercise that will make all the difference in your daily life. We know it may seem like you don't have time to breathe with all the hours you're putting in, but we're sure you can squeeze it in on your bus ride to the hotel, on your way to the gym, or while having a nice cup of coffee with a friend.

What are you grateful for?

I know it's not always easy to say it, but think of one person who makes you happy in life. If you didn't have this person in your life, how different would your life be?

When you answer these questions, all you need to do is set your timer for two minutes and start writing without lifting your pen off the paper. Two minutes is all I ask of you. Write everything that you are grateful for in your life. When the timer goes off, stop writing.

Once you complete this exercise, go back to the beginning of your list, and next to each item, write **WHY?**

Now, for the next two days, focus only on the positive in your life and only count your blessings. Think of what you are grateful for and you already have, not what you want or don't have yet.

Focus on the abundance you already have that is present in everything you do: while walking down the street, driving, interacting with family, friends, and strangers in your daily life.

When you notice yourself gossiping or criticizing, consciously dismiss such behavior. Just think of it as a game, as if you weren't allowed to dwell on any negative situations.

Before you go to bed, go back to your journal and write your observations.

Write a list of tiny miracles that remind you how wonderful it is to be alive today, not a decade ago, or in the future. Right at this very moment.

Next time you experience a crappy day, look at your list and remember how wonderful life can be and how amazing you are.

Now, imagine finally getting what you're after, what your heart so ardently yearns for.

How does that make you feel? What feelings overcome your entire being?

Stay in that state, enjoy it to the fullest, and embrace the upbeat energy coming your way.

Now, *Skybabe,* open your journal and write your heart out.

- **What's something you witnessed recently that reminded you that life is good?**

- **What's one thing you've enjoyed about doing your job recently?**

- **What made you laugh or smile today?**

- **What's a hard lesson you were grateful to learn?**

- **How was today better than yesterday?**

- **What have you seen in nature recently that made you feel happy, peaceful or free?**

- **Have you had a chance to help someone today, and how did that make you feel?**

- **What's something you look forward to in the future?**

- **Who is someone that really listens when you talk, and how does that affect you?**

- **What's an aspect of your physical health that you feel grateful for?**

- **What's improved about your life from this time last year?**

- **What book or podcast affected your life for the better recently?**

List three things you have now that you prayed you would have ten years ago.

1.
2.
3.

12

Skybabe Saves the Day

LANGUAGE IS A DIVINE GIFT

With languages, you are at home anywhere.
Edmund de Waal

Munchkin,

Did you understand what that passenger in front of you wanted? *Agua*? Ah, okay! We'll get him his water in a second. Do you speak Spanish? No? But you understood him well. And I've heard you talk to him for a bit. *Muy bien!*

How many languages do you speak, *Skybabe*?

We were a big, loud group of young people. Dancers and musicians, on a tour, taking part in festivals all over Mexico for one whole month. Our boarding, with all those bags, instruments and costumes, couldn't pass unnoticed at the airport. I was 24 then, and this was my first flight. Ever. Yet, in just a few years' time, I would be flying more than any average person in the world. This trip was special because it was like a christening experience in the sky for me.

Talk about life changes. In less than three years.

As a group of around thirty restless souls—with the noise we made mingling in the aisle, trying to figure out the best seating for all—we annoyed the hell out of flight attendants.

But not Carlos. All groomed up with his dark brown hair and beautifully straight, sparkling white teeth, Carlos approached us enthusiastic yet patient and calm.

I passed by him and glanced at his name tag. "*Hola!*"

"*Hola!*" Carlos said to me with a big smile.

The second thing that caught my eye were the little flags below his name tag. I quickly figured out that all those represented the languages he spoke. Impressive, I thought. But, when he found out where we were from, he instantly transformed into a chatterbox, all cute and funny, pronouncing popular phrases in my native language with pure perfection.

As someone who doesn't just love, but adores studying languages, and who has become a teacher of one, I have a huge respect for polyglots.

Since this was my first time traveling abroad, I never really had much chance to talk to foreigners. But seeing Carlos, so confident and in his element, made me realize that speaking foreign languages was my ticket to the world. And I knew it would open new doors for me. My entire life I lived in books and movies, wondering what it would be like to understand everything without the subtitles. To be able to absorb the original writing and understand it in my own way without anyone standing between the author and me. Would it be exactly the same? Would I have the identical feeling or would it be better?

Why does it even matter when you can simply read the translation?

Well, because ...

> A different language is a different vision of life.
> *Federico Fellini*

Mr. Fellini, I couldn't agree more. Language is the mirror of the reality of a society or one's life and as that reality changes, so does the language. Words and the language depict culture, customs, and distinct traits of a certain nation. And there are words that exist only in a specific language, because they represent something unique from that culture. That's where you have difficulties translating those special words.

Can you relate, *Skybabe*?

Remember a time when you tried to explain a word from your language to someone, but after numerous tries, you simply gave up because it was impossible?

Mate from Argentina is simply *mate*. *Ikigai* from Japan will always be *ikigai*. And how about *umami*, *saudade*, or *dolce far niente?* I bet you have endless examples, *Skybabe*. Send us yours!

VARICELLA, BABY!

"*Signorina, signorina, scusi!*" I heard a loud voice from behind as I rushed down to the galley to collect more casseroles and continue the service.

We still had around two hours to get to Venice and one full service to deliver. The flight was full, as usual, but what surprised me was that many of the passengers on board came from Bangladesh and spoke Italian. Some form of Italian, that is.

So did my panicking passenger.

I had to stop and check what was going on, although I was in a hurry and pretty determined to dart through the aisle, as the little Tasmanian Devil would.

I turned around and saw a man pointing at his body, repeating, *"Varicella! Varicella!"*

Saying the same word over and over again, he tried to explain that his body was itchy and red. I gave a little whisk of a smile and continued on. And then he barked, *"Varicella! Varicella!"*

While studying Latin for six years back in high school and university, I would often ask myself, "Where the heck would I ever use all those quotes, irregular verbs, and vocabulary?"

And *voilà!* This situation was the answer.

I knew varicella—a highly contagious disease—meant chickenpox, and I was grateful that none of the people around us knew it. There weren't many Italians on the flight, either. Otherwise, the panic in the cabin would have easily spread like the plague, so I decided to keep it as discreet as possible while investigating the situation further.

I glanced at the man who sure looked flustered, but didn't seem that serious to me. He kept repeating the same old thing as I tried to get more information from him. His Italian was poor, and he didn't seem to understand me well.

And then it hit me like a ton of bricks! Holy Moly, I never had chickenpox in my life! *If what he's saying is true, I'm done. What do I do?*

Although now I started panicking, too, I wasn't quite sure that what he was saying was right. I was thinking about plan A, B, C and finally, I had no plan. Paging a doctor on board? Calling medical assistance? Diversion for chickenpox? *Hmm.*

My spinning mind was restless. Considering all the options, I finally chose Option M.

M.A.N.

A male colleague.

I invited the other senior who worked with me in the cabin to talk to the guy and give me his opinion. Once he arrived, he spent less than two minutes talking. In a matter of seconds, the passenger just sank into his seat in between his wife and two sons.

What my colleague did was what no knowledge of language could help with. He spoke at the same frequency as the passenger, but to his panic, my colleague responded with firmness and assertiveness. There were no scary words or threats. My colleague's body language and tone were enough to shut the Varicella victim down.

Wow! And all this time I was trying to figure out the way to communicate with words and all the languages I knew.

It was useless. Useless, I tell ya!

The only thing helpful in such a situation was BODY LANGUAGE. I knew it was powerful, but I didn't know it was that potent. And so I figured the whole scenario was the product of this passenger's imagination, fear or some fake story he made up to get more free stuff from the airline.

Really, dude? Varicella? I don't think so.

After the flight, I stayed with the thought and the fact that 93 percent of communication exists through body language — the nonverbal communication. Only seven percent is verbal. This was mind-blowing to me. And it still is. Especially to the language lover who believed in the power of words over anything.

On the other side of the spectrum, in the industry of *Skybabes*, a smile as part of our body language is the *firstest*, the *mostest* and the *importantest* asset out of all.

What a smile can do, nothing else can: introduce yourself and your energy to strangers, open doors, make somebody feel welcome, melt hearts, quiet down a baby's cry, calm the tone of a discussion, earn respect, make someone fall in love with you, resolve a conflict, etc.

And here I'm talking about a genuine heartfelt smile.

I'm sure, *Skybabe*, you can easily differentiate a sincere smile from a fake one—the one widely spread in the customer service industry.

I know I must sound like a broken record at this point, but I truly believe that a smile is a universal language everyone understands. On every continent, country or flight you do.

Be smart about it and use it often. **It's free,** and it doesn't take much effort. And while you make someone else feel better, **you'll start feeling better, too!**

OH, YOU'RE A FLIGHT ATTENDANT? YOU MUST SPEAK MANY LANGUAGES!

And before you can blink your lustrous eyelashes, you courteously pretend you didn't hear this question for the millionth time since you began flying. I'll be the first one to raise my hand and admit that I thought all *Skybabes* had at least three or four languages in their pockets.

One for every occasion.

But in my long flying career, I learned this to be far from the truth. I've seen anything from barely speaking proper English *Skybabes* to the remarkable examples of polyglots. Just like Carlos from the beginning of this chapter, who later became a friend and a great host in his house in Mexico City.

Now, boo, let's look at the facts. The estimated number of languages in the world is around 7,100. The most widely spoken languages are English, Mandarin Chinese, Hindi, Spanish, French, Arabic, Bengali, Russian, Portuguese, and Indonesian. Only three percent of the world's population speaks over four languages and less than one percent speaks five languages fluently. Although not everyone is a language lover among *Skybabes*, the aviation industry is a fertile soil for developing your language skills. Such an international environment, both with colleagues and passengers, gives you an incredible opportunity to practice, learn and explore. The mixes I've seen during my career were astounding: Brazilians who spoke fluent Japanese, Africans who spoke Mandarin, Chinese who spoke Portuguese, etc. I've seen it all. Or almost all.

But let me tell you about that one time my polyglot tongue got tied. Or should I say, got me out of trouble.

After my marvelous adventure through the rainforests of West Africa, a few days later, I landed in Beijing. This flight was doubly special to me because, first, I'd never been to Beijing, even though I'd been to China before and had visited Shanghai many times, and second, because I'd finally get to visit the Great Wall of China. Another world wonder crossed off my list.

So, the moment we reached our fancy hotel, I took the names and room numbers of the crew members who wanted to go with me. We arranged a tour that would take us to the Great Wall, the Forbidden City, the Tiananmen Square and a few other famous spots. So, early the next morning, we put our hiking shoes on, wrapped ourselves in warm jackets and shawls, and headed to one of the greatest Modern World wonders.

Now, *Skybabe,* if you've never been to China, particularly Beijing, you probably don't know the vastness of the place. Everything is huge. I mean *huge.* Which differs greatly from other Asian countries. But in Beijing, wherever you go, you're surrounded by rivers of people. And that's why I decided to get the earliest bus possible to avoid the crowds and experience the serenity of the Great Wall.

After two hours, we arrived at the main entrance. Since it was still quite early, our bus driver managed to drop us off right at the entrance gate. As we said goodbye to him, I made sure to take his number and license plate, just in case. I made a mental note of the bus parking position on the empty parking lot and carried on.

I had to pinch myself a few times as I set foot on this adventurous wall hike. As I strolled among extraordinary watchtowers, absorbing the picturesque Wall and indulging in the breathtaking scenery, I remembered reading about this architectural marvel in one of my favorite childhood books, *Wonders of the World,* by Roland Gööck. Miles of stunning terrain and breathtaking scenery followed us as we hiked the steep steps, enjoying the splendid views of the rolling hills and color-changing leaves.

At some point, the group parted, and we all agreed to meet at the main gate at 1 p.m. sharp. As I made my way down through the rivers of people, the tranquil, majestic Great Wall no longer seemed so inviting. I gushed down the cobblestone path as fast as I could, but the moment I reached the parking lot, shock almost choked me.

Our tiny bus was nowhere to be found.

Gobbled up by an ocean of cars, trucks and school buses, it simply disappeared. To add to my shock, none of my colleagues were anywhere near. I swallowed a hard lump in my throat and went to search for our bus driver. Frantically, I looked left and right, desperate to find a familiar face or anyone who spoke English.

To my luck, a group of Japanese tourists that had just arrived was getting off the bus opposite me. I opened the map, took a deep breath and, with the biggest smile, set my foot forward to ask for help.

Yes, *Skybabe,* I was in the middle of Beijing, speaking Japanese to a Chinese tour guide who then translated my words into Mandarin to another bus driver who knew where my driver was. *Whew!*

The guy who helped me was so sweet and kind that within minutes, I was standing in front of my bus. Thinking of that scene now still gives me the chills. It was a scary moment, but my *Skybabe* spirit kept me sane. I knew things would be okay in the end. And as soon as I realized that all my colleagues had made it in one piece, I exhaled a sigh of relief. Laughing and chitter-chattering, we were soon on our way to the Forbidden City.

PROTECT YOUR INNER WORLD

She stood in the storm and when the wind did not blow her way,
she adjusted her sails.
Elizabeth Edwards

13

Are You There, God? It's Us, Skybabes

Don't You Just Hate It When Shit Hits the Fan

Defeat is a state of mind. No one is ever defeated
until defeat has been accepted as a reality.
Bruce Lee

Hey sunshine,

There comes a time in every *Skybabe's* life when you have to face the inevitable: Yes, the job's awesome, but what if something goes wrong?

I know, I know, it sounds crazy. Anything can happen, but *nothing* will happen. I'd like to think the same way. But at times, I felt more like a scared little mouse than an elephant. I have to admit that when I flew in my uniform, I felt like I had that superhero cape fluttering behind me, confident I could do things only Superman can. But when I travel as a passenger, I'm as fearful as Clark Kent. Just as any other passenger on board.

Look, we're not here to teach you safety and security. But sometimes you really have to trust your gut when dealing with the unexpected.

Frankly speaking, most of my flights were safe and sound. Apart from a few crazy dreads here and there, most of the time I went to bed with a smile on my face, no matter how exhausting the flight may have been. There were times when I lost passengers on board due to heart failure, after many, many tries to revive them. Or a time when we encountered hydraulic problems and had to land with only one engine on. I'd experienced aborted landings, return to field, fuel jettison, thunderstorms and lightning strikes, severe turbulence, and a disruptive passenger attack. And I still went to bed feeling safe because the airline industry has one of the best safety systems in the world. And when you work for a well-established, reputable airline, you're pretty much in good hands. Or at least, you want to believe so.

And as I said, Superman and I were best friends. But there was one time I will never forget. The one time I thought shit was truly about to hit the fan.

I remember my flight to Côte d'Ivoire, that had several stops on the way. On our final leg, the Captain informed us that a severe storm was approaching our destination and that we would have to land before the cyclone hit the ground. This kept us safe from diverting to another place and all the complications no one wanted to deal with: further delays, roster changes, and even more chaos.

Usually, the descent takes approximately half an hour, but due to certain circumstances it can last much shorter or much longer, depending on the weather, traffic density, and onboard situations such as sick passenger emergencies.

And that day, we didn't have half an hour to get ready. We didn't even get ten minutes. Within seconds of Captain's announcement, we were expected to be strapped in our seats, ready to land. No chit-chat, no extra drinks delivered to passengers. Just plain and simple, "Cabin crew, take your seats *now!*"

The crew did their duties. We all secured the cabin and took our seats.

But the only thing *il comandante* forgot to mention (a teeny tiny detail) was that in order to land, we would have to go through the mighty storm for a nanoscopic bit of time and experience a hell of a turbulence.

All was fine until the initial phase of the approach—the moment that engraved itself in my brain without ever getting invited. It seemed as if we raced against Mother Nature who sure would emerge victorious in this encounter. But when you fly with an adventurous soul who's a tad bit crazy (a.k.a. our Captain for the day), you persuade yourself it's for the best.

A bit of a daredevil!

He kind of reminded me of my grandpa, an air force pilot who once flew his plane under a bridge to escape a Nazi fighter jet. Look, my grandpa wasn't a daredevil. He was plain crazy! But that's another story.

I passed my checks to the Purser and hurried to the back of the aircraft. I sat in the jumpseat next to a sweet girl who was covering the rear door and had just recently started flying. Yes, she was sweet. And frightened.

Just as I buckled myself up securely, the turbulence hit the plane, and all hell broke loose—hatracks opening, bags falling out, passengers screaming in horror. Hands lifted in the air, mouth open, murmuring prayers to God, gods, deities, and spirits—the whole shebang.

I turned to my left to see my senior colleague panting. Fingers covered his mouth as if to hold off a scream that would soon break free from his throat. I turned to the right to see the sweet girl cringing. A panicked expression flittered across her beautiful face.

He was soon praying to Allah. She was calling out Jesus. The lady in front of us called Shiva to come to her rescue. And I'm pretty sure I heard someone yell Buddha's name, too.

Shite. This didn't look good.

Even the Superman in me started shittin' his pants. What the hell was going on?

With my heart in my mouth, I drew in a stuttered gasp and smoothed the hem of my skirt. Warning bells went off, but I shook my head. *No way. We're going to be fine.*

You know what they say about your environment? You are who you spend your time with. Well, at that moment I could have easily panicked, but I wasn't giving in.

At least for some time.

As we hit another air pocket, the aircraft dropped another few hundred feet, and my stomach churned. Think of the scariest roller coaster you've ever ridden, then multiply that by a hundred. I'm not even joking. My palms were sweating, but I needed to keep my composure. Another drop and I gasped. My muscles froze. Was I the only crazy person thinking we'd get out of this alive?

Panic swelled up inside me and in my mind, I had already started to run, scream and shout, but on the outside, I somehow managed to keep my cool. I imagined having that parachute strapped to my back in case doors flew open and we all went flying.

Amid all the horror, the interphone rang. The sound of hope. Relief. Escape. Or was it? By the chime and the lights flashing on the indicator above me, I knew it was the Captain calling. The girl mending the door was the one who had to answer it. I signaled with my head for her to pick it up. She looked at me as if her words escaped her and drove all the breathable air from her body. Lifting the handle, she turned to me and shoved the phone into my hand, her clammy palms leaving a visible trace over my skirt. Seconds later, she went limp, then burst into tears.

Despite her reaction, I kept my chin up and put the handset to my ear.

"Hey guys, how's it going back there?"

A flamboyant, carefree voice said on the other side of the line. The Captain. The voice of relief and sudden calmness that overcame me amidst all the chaos I was feeling inside and out.

I told you he was crazy! How can you be calm in such a situation? Well, that's why he was the one flying the plane. He knew his shit.

The moment I heard the Captain's voice, I knew things were going to be okay. He was cool and calm and just wanted to check on us as the tail of the aircraft is usually hit hardest during the storm. His tone of voice told me we were okay and that we would land soon. Luckily, we were faster than the storm and we made it in one piece.

A few excruciatingly long minutes later, we were on land, safe and sound. The Captain took a quick walk through the cabin to make sure every single passenger was fine. In awe, people followed him with their wide-open eyes, touching him as if he were some kind of superhero who came to save their lives.

Even now as I write this, I get goosebumps just thinking about it. He really was Superman. He was super cool and super amazing, and it showed. Because he cared.

Thank you, Captain!

14

One Powerful Skybabe

AIN'T THAT TRAVEL RESILIENCE MUSCLE AS STRONG AS A ROCK SOMETIMES

Do not judge me by my successes, judge me by how
many times I fell down and got back up again.
Nelson Mandela

WHAT DO I DO NOW?

Dance is a form of art.

A sort of expression that allows you to be creative in magnificent new ways. It brings people together, lets you escape the stresses of everyday life and helps you maintain great mental and emotional health. And it provides a sense of community with people that have similar interests and passions. It keeps you happy, satisfied and calm that no matter how stressful or frustrating a situation may be, you still find a way out.

And as I disembarked the first flight I'd ever taken in my life, I was about to be put to the test for everything I had learned about being calm in a stressful situation.

· ♥ · ♥ · ♥ · ♥ · ♥ ·

I stood next to the baggage carousel, waiting for my suitcase to arrive. For the last half an hour, I waited patiently, thinking it probably got stuck somewhere on its way to me. The belt kept moving, but I stood motionless, staring without blinking.

The carousel had probably made over thirty rounds, bringing the same bags (the ones that no one ever seems to claim) coming from London to Mexico City. If my eyes could miraculously pass and sneak in through that black rubber curtain, I would run inside and only then could I convince myself that my suitcase was *really* missing and that this all wasn't just someone's grim joke.

Everybody else in my group took their bags and started leaving. Out of two suitcases I brought with me on this *long* trip to Mexico, I was now left with one which had nothing but my dance costumes in it.

What shall I do? Walk the streets dressed like Carmen, the Gypsy of Seville?

Tears rolled down my cheeks. First, I felt nauseous from the landing. Now, this.

I was devastated. It was my first flying experience and just the thought of not having my clothes at all, or the possibility of losing everything that I had brought with me that time, made me sink even deeper. I believed it was the end of the world, not knowing that lost baggage is a regular occurrence in any airline. I already imagined my bag being swallowed by crocodiles, or thrown in some dirty, long-forgotten corner of a warehouse, misplaced on the way by some major glitch in the system.

It took quite some time to understand how things work—to always bring a few necessities with me when I travel and have a Plan B in case something goes wrong.

Mind you, I was not *Skybabe* at the time, but this was the first occasion where my Travel Resilience Muscle (TRM) started to get stronger. This was actually the first time I discovered I had it.

Getting my suitcase back took longer than usual, since I was on the go with my group, traveling around the country. We changed many states, cities and addresses in just a few short days, but finally, I received it. What a relief!

What I learned then was to always do the best I can with what I have at the moment. There's no other way, really. So, whenever I travel, I arm myself with plenty of positive energy and a carry-on full of bare necessities, believing that everything somehow gets solved in the end. And I'm quite certain I kept that belief for life.

THE CHARMS OF FLYING ON STANDBY TICKETS

You know how it goes. You check the load on your phone and see how many passengers checked in already. Five seats left in the premium cabins, a few seats in Economy. Lovely jubbly! Now you're even eyeing those two empty seats at the back. It all seems good and you smile. But then, you worm your way up to the counter, with cold sweat trickling down your back. Deep down, you're already on board, but there's a payload restriction. They might accept you, but not your bags. Or they might not accept you at all. So, you start cursing the day you decided to pack that giant suitcase of yours. They'll choose a staff member who's traveling with their carry-on. You know it and your stomach tightens.

"Come back in 45minutes, Miss. Then we'll be able to tell you if we've accepted you on the flight. There's no need to stand here and tap your toes."

Right.

Well, I wanted to say, "Why the heck don't you check me in now?! The flight obviously has seats available and I'm your colleague, for goodness' sake! Why do you want to prolong my misery?" But I do none of that, because every time I tried to be firm with the check-in staff, it hit me back. So instead, I nod, take my two enormous suitcases in my hands, turn around and walk away from the check-in counter.

As usual, the regular passengers stand in the line, staring. They notice there's something special about this girl—me. First, she went to inquire at a different counter and now she's coming back with her unchecked bags. What's going on there?

There is no point in going anywhere now, because at Jakarta International Airport there is actually nowhere to go (at least at the time). So I sit on an agonizingly uncomfortable wooden bench facing the check-in counter and the clock on the wall.

Sound familiar, *Skybabe*?

Time passes at a snail's pace and I constantly look at my phone, my watch, and the clock. As if one of them is not enough, right? The last few minutes are approaching. The worst ones. As I sit and wait, tapping my foot on the floor, I have this nerve-wrecking feeling inside me.

Yikes!

The one nobody likes, and nobody except *Skybabe* knows it. In your head and your heart, you're battling hope and fear. Fear is making you plot plans in case you don't get on that flight. And hope is still energizing you and not leaving you until the end. Because, you never know! Miracles *do* happen! And you might get that boarding pass after all!

Although there are still a few minutes left, I stand up and get myself closer to the counter, just in case they forgot who I was—to show them I was still alive and kicking. *Hello!* In front of their eyes. They call me out and regretfully say they cannot accept me on the flight. There is nothing they can do. They've tried already. Payload restrictions.

"But you don't understand. I have two connecting flights after this one and an important event to attend. Please, help me. Is there any way I can go via Singapore instead?"

I get another firm NO.

And the saga continues. One in the line of many standby chronicles. Some that ended happily, and some that made me cry. But when I remember them now, I smile, although then it seemed my entire world came crashing down.

I had another fourteen hours to go until the next flight that didn't seem too promising, either. I was exhausted, since I had already come on a flight from the island of Manado in Indonesia. I had a wonderful time, but coming back to Europe now seemed more complicated and challenging than I first thought it would be. The airport had hardly anything except those ridiculously uncomfortable wooden benches. With no back support.

Argh!

Aimlessly roaming through the airport with my trolley and two large suitcases packed on top of each other, I thought about what to do next. People kept looking at me. My long blonde hair, blue eyes and my height, although average in Europe, seemed too unusual for them. Just a week ago, I would have gladly accepted being in their photos with a huge smile on my face, but right now I was furious and had no patience for anyone. I sat on the bench and waited. And waited. And waited some more. After a few hours, one of the ground staff saw me struggling to sleep, so he showed me to a hotel I could use to refresh myself.

Even though I had to pay a full day rate, I still decided to go as I needed to rest. That shower after the humidity and stickiness together with a much-needed one-hour sleep was worth all the money in the world. Refreshed and somewhat rested, I went back to the very same check-in counter. And the familiar story began. The same anxious feeling. The sweating. The hope and the fear. All over again.

This flight was overbooked, but God knows why, I was a lot more patient and composed this time. I waited until the very end, until I surrendered. ***Whatever happens, happens.*** And then I heard a voice. "Miss, Miss, come here! We can check you in, but you need to run to the gate *now*! It is the very last gate!"

A sigh of relief broke out from my chest, followed by a HUGE THANK YOU to the check-in staff. I thanked the Universe, Mother Earth, and all the galaxies yet unheard of as I grabbed that boarding pass and started to run. And as it usually happens, Murphy's law kicked in and I was on my way to another one of many monumental challenges of life. Hundreds of meters of airport terminal hallway kept me away from my goal—to board that plane and get home as soon as possible.

My trolley broke while running, so I had to carry it in my arms. I knew I'd have sore muscles the next day, but I couldn't think about anything else but that gate. With sweat rushing down my neck, sides and back, running as if my life depended on it, I reached the gate.

Just. In. Time.

The last few passengers boarded in front of me and once I crossed the air bridge and stepped on the aircraft, my shoulders dropped with relief. *Phew!*

That feeling of releasing the tension and anxiety in a split second is something *Skybabes* who love to travel on standby tickets could teach as relaxation techniques on retreats.

Inhale. Exhale. Let go.

I went to my seat and closed my eyes, only to wake up just before landing.

The other two flights were as risky as the first one to get on to, but the lucky star followed my way, so I succeeded. I was optimistic and determined to reach my final destination and attend that event. I didn't know how, but I knew I'd get there. And I did. But I was so exhausted from my endless trip that the moment I lay down in my bed, I started crying like a baby.

After only thirty hours of traveling.

I know with certainty that not everyone is built to withhold this kind of stress, where you need to stay flexible in changing travel plans last minute while making the best out of any situation. But with the perspective I have now, I think that standby traveling experience helped me become a more resilient person. A person who can face unusual situations with incredible creativity to find new solutions.

THINGS GET BETTER

You're planning to go to Rome, but somehow you end up in Venice. There, you're assisted by a cute Italian train station staff who helps you lift that 29kg suitcase on the train followed by his charming, *"Arrivederci, bella!"* only to reach your desired place after changing one more train and a bus. You arrive with a 15-hour delay, dragging your suitcases over the rich Italian soil surrounded by beautiful olive trees. You feel like Cameron Diaz in *The Holiday*. When she arrives in the village on her heels with heavy bags, she can barely move over the deep snow. And yes, she's a bit lost and tired, but happy.

How about this, *Skybabe?* You're headed to Jamaica via Fort Lauderdale to attend a wedding. The US airport security announces there would be a delay in delivering bags, since they are about to do a random baggage security check. You and your friend lose a connecting flight with a different airline and the check-in staff cannot do anything about it. Maybe only transfer you to another flight that leaves in two days, since everything until then is full.

As if! Zero initiative to help.

And the wedding is in two days! So, what do you do? You sit for a bit on your suitcase, cry it out and then those crazy bingo thoughts start coming up. That TRM gets fired up all over again.

Your friend's creative mind starts rolling. You both run as fast as you can to the other terminal and skip the line with a loud, "Excuse me, pardon me, I am sorry!" and get to that one *amazingly amazing* check-in staff on the other side of the counter who wants to do everything in his power to help you get to Jamaica on time.

Still, instead of Kingston, Jamaica, you end up in Atlanta, but that's okay! From there, you take another flight, and another car ride and soon enough, after over 24 hours of traveling, you get to Negril, Jamaica, only to learn that your bags are missing. Oh, well! Here we go again! At least, you're safe and sound and you made it to the wedding. That counts!

Or how about coming to the airport all relaxed and certain you would check in quickly, do a bit of Duty Free shopping and head to the aircraft, since you're on your annual leave ticket which, by the book, guarantees you a seat? But then, you find out that the book has been written in the language you apparently don't quite understand and you get taken off the flight. As a result, you lose your $500 connecting flight from Seattle to Denver, local transportation, a day of accommodation and the first day of yoga retreat you were planning to attend in Boulder, Colorado — the greenest city in America.

For two long hours, you fight for your right at the counter, until that same flight you were supposed to be on departs. Disappointed and miserable, you go back home to work on Plan B and return to the airport the next day with high hopes that everything would be solved somehow.

Tears. *Again*. Here and there. And then buckets and gallons of tears running down your cheeks as you book another connecting flight to Denver. With a broken toe in heavy hiking shoes, you finally reach Boulder. You practice ZEN for a week surrounded by stunning nature, mountains, hiking trails, a variety of vegan food and yoga classes that you haven't experienced anywhere before. What happens then? You forget about all the misery you went through to get there.

Or how about being stranded with your friend in La Habana, Cuba, trying to get to Europe through another connecting flight? Flights are canceled left and right due to terrible weather and, as a result, ours is overbooked. No Wi-Fi at the time anywhere at the airport (yes, true story—the charms of Cuba). But then, like pulling a rabbit out of a hat, we find a staff member who's kind enough to hear us out. Maybe the fact that we spoke Spanish had something to do with it, but this wonderful man let us use his office computer that he reopened just for us. We manage to rebook our tickets to Paris instead of Madrid. The situation is tight. La Habana is always swarming with staff members on standby, but we're still hopeful. We get our boarding passes and board last. We get separate seats, but we're on board! YES! *Thank you, Universe!*

I sigh in relief and sink into my seat. Then, out of nowhere, I hear my name on the passenger announcement system. A ground staff member is approaching my seat with a French family behind him. The family is also traveling standby, and they were accepted right after us. Oh, no! I'll be removed from the flight! This is *not* happening.

By some miracle, and good fortune, an extra seat in Business Class appears. One of the family members zooms by me to get to Business Class and the rest of them are already seated. I'm still in my seat. The doors are closed for departure. Hell, yeah! *Chocolat chaud,* I'm still going to have some of you on this flight!

We reach Paris and . . . need I say it again? We run to the other terminal to catch the flight to our final destination, but before we could get on board, we had to rebook our tickets. TRM in action again! I don't know how, but we made it just in time, even on this occasion.

I forgot to mention the weather catastrophes. Storms in India, bad weather in Canada, volcano eruptions and ashes in Bali and all the waiting at the airports, sleeping on uncomfortable benches, sitting on the floor, spending unplanned extra nights in cities you would never plan to stay in, even ending up sharing a room with people you don't know.

Then again, once you get the hang of standby tickets and start traveling with an open mind, you'll see that sometimes you'll get on a flight, although you gave it no chance (since you were only the 18th staff member on the list). Somehow you end up in New York JFK just in time to meet your friend coming from LaGuardia Airport for a cup of coffee at Penn Station Starbucks before heading to your Airbnb in Brooklyn.

So, how about you? If you're already *Skybabe*, have you started using your standby tickets for traveling? How's it going so far?

Finally, I would like to express my deepest gratitude and say THANK YOU to all the check-in and ground personnel I have encountered on my travels. Some would do absolutely everything in their power to help, some couldn't care less; some were fair, and others were just following the rules. Regardless of my personal experience, I always choose to believe that people are willing to help one another. More often than not, it worked, and I believe that many times my mindset, positive attitude, and resilience brought me to all the places I've been to around the world.

15

Nobody Messes with Skybabe

HOW TO DEAL WITH STRESS WHILE FLYING

*If you cannot find peace within yourself, you will
never find it anywhere else.*
Marvin Gaye

Hey cutie pie,

Shit happens. Rosters change, flights get delayed, passengers die. And you are the one who has to deal with it all. But sometimes, no matter how hard you try to keep those high vibes in the air around you and your safety bubble safe from bursting, something happens that pushes that lever just a tad bit higher and you suddenly lose your marbles.

Imagine this.

You're on a full afternoon flight. Passengers are swarming like ants on a hot summer day, waiting for you to serve their fancy lunch after takeoff. Kids are screaming, engines are blaring, your junior colleague is brand new to galley operation. To add to your misery, you are one crew short because of the last-minute changes and as you sit in your seat waiting for that seatbelt sign to go off, you brace yourself. Not for impact, but for the whole hullabaloo you're about to experience.

This is not me telling you funny stories. This is *real*.

Skybabe, sometimes you'll find yourself smooth sailing across the skies, enjoying your virgin Bloody Mary in the First Class galley, casually chatting with passengers. And then, there will be times when a 12-hour flight turns into a non-stop marathon. Because there's no clock on the wall that says you're done. And sometimes, when no one is watching, you'll be the one not to take a break. A major slap on the wrist. This is illegal by all international standards and you should take your break time seriously. Never skip it, no matter how busy you are. The rest of the crew will survive without you. No need to hover above and micromanage. You're not a helicopter quenching forest fires, you're *Skybabe*, aware of what's really worth her energy.

How many times have you left the aircraft thinking, "Worst twelve hours of my life?" Or said, "Sure, great!" to a passenger or colleague when all you wanted was to throw them out of the plane. People can literally go on your nerves, but you can't wear your heart on your sleeve, *Skybabe*. Not in our industry.

Back to my dreary afternoon flight. We survived the three hellish hours, and the passengers were now disembarking. As I greeted every customer with a pleasant goodbye, one particular passenger abruptly stopped in front of me and shot me a furious glance.

Still poking his angry finger at me, he glared at me without blinking. "You bitch!"

And then he exploded.

A barrage of pretty useful swear words came out of his mouth, some of which I'd never heard but wish I could have written down. I stood, watching, unable to process the anger unfolding in front of me. What the hell was he talking about? My nails cut into the heel of my hand as I tightened it. I managed to keep my poker face and stay cool, but in my mind, I'd already killed him ten times in ten different ways.

"Because of you, we're late." He barked in anger. "I want to complain!"

I still wondered in bewilderment how this was all my fault. It wasn't like I was the one flying the plane or having the power to decide when we would *actually* depart. Plus, the flight had already been delayed when we got to our briefing room, so no surprises there.

"What do you mean, sir?" I asked, still confused as I watched him hiss like a cornered serpent in front of me.

As he continued blabbering, I learned that because of the flight length, he wasn't able to finish watching his movie. And since I was the one who switched off the in-flight entertainment system before landing, he was pissed off.

Now, *Skybabe*, at this point, you're probably wondering what I'm talking about. At the time (read: fifteen years ago), when ancient in-flight entertainment was still a big deal, we used cassettes that we distributed on demand in our premium cabins. Cassettes sometimes didn't work and you always, *always,* had to rewind them for the crew overtaking the plane even if you had a flight full of creeps spitting in your face. Fun times!

Okay. That wasn't a big deal. So, a passenger yelled at me. I could handle it. And I did. As professionally and calmly as I could. After all, this was what I was trained to do—handle a conflict peacefully and professionally.

But sometimes, you encounter passengers who are . . . I'm not sure what to call them. Oh yeah, jerks.

On one particular flight, when everything that could go wrong did, I found myself in the middle of chaos. I was performing CPR on a cardiac arrest passenger, desperately waiting for my colleague to bring the defibrillator, so we had a higher chance of saving this passenger's life. As I removed the jewelry and placed the pads on the man's bare chest, before I even pressed the "shock" button, I heard the inconceivable. "Where's my gin and tonic?"

With my beating heart and a sweaty forehead, I looked up to see a nosy prick towering over me and my dying patient, asking for a drink.

Thank God for colleagues with common sense and great team spirit. I'll forever be grateful to a fellow *Skydude* who handled the situation more than well as I fought for the life of my elderly passenger in the aisle.

And then, I found myself flying over the Atlantic when another passenger complained about his seat not working properly. And on top of that, he was seated next to a snoring passenger.

Not my fault.

At this point, you know that full flights mean that even onboard cockroaches fight for space. Of course, I did everything I could to make him feel better, but he still wanted to sit in a new seat because he felt too crowded by other passengers because of his size.

Entirely his fault.

Anyway, since he still insisted on being reseated, I offered him a nice cozy corner by the lavatory where he could stretch his legs. Or perhaps a wing would have been even more spacious.

And let's not forget the ones who stare, tsk, tap, and poke at you during meal service.

Ah, the joys of flying!

So, how do *you* deal with stress, *Skybabe*?

Are you impulsive and irrational or calm and patient? Have you ever asked yourself why you get stressed often?

Imagine a day when you're tired and easily irritated but cannot figure out why. You know you're not mad at anyone, but people still notice your frustration and start asking questions, telling you to relax and calm down.

But you don't need their advice. So, you get even more annoyed.

What you really need is to be left alone.

All by yourself. To sit in silence and **become aware of your emotions, feelings, and your presence.**

As flight attendants, we all have dirty little secrets our passengers don't know about. But one thing's for sure: we all carry a smile or, better yet, a facial expression that conceals our emotions. When we're happy, angry, or exhausted, when we welcome them on board, or simply want to tell them to *eff* off, we always smile. And that's hard.

It's exhausting, but it's part of the job and we simply have to do it.

Now imagine you're boarding a full flight all by yourself and your angry passenger hasn't even stepped on the plane, yet he's already yelling at you. They lost his luggage, of course. He missed his connection, and he's hungry as a wolf. You keep listening and absorbing all the lovely words that are coming your way. You were trained to stay calm in stressful situations, but you've had a lousy day and you won't take shit from anyone. Even from this monster who you'd gladly send off to a raging typhoon if you could.

Between outward smiles and inward screams, you're fighting a silent battle deep inside, trying hard to remain professional while giving the jerk a mental middle finger. Your pride is hurt, your identity threatened and you're starting to lose your buttons. You're boiling with fury as blood rushes to your head, but you know you have to stay cool, calm, and collected.

I know this rarely happens, boo, but these days are real and you shouldn't be ashamed of them. You are a real person. A human being with feelings and a big heart. And sometimes, no matter how difficult and disrespectful passengers are, you have to swallow hard and take the punch. Especially when you have an unsupportive senior who'd rather suck up to passengers than stand behind her crew. But those occasions are rare, too.

Still, there is a way to control your anger, and it all depends on what you want at that particular moment. If you can predict how you might react, you can learn how to respond to such situations in a peaceful manner.

Notice how I said, **respond** and not react?

Over the years, I've learned that reacting to life's daily frustrations only made me more stressed. But I've also learned how to be prepared so that I can control my behavior if a situation like this occurs again.

I learned that skipping meals makes me feel sluggish and nervous, socializing for too long makes me tired and anxious, and working long hours without taking breaks, (thinking that I'm fine), causes burnout which ultimately leads to lack of patience and ability to focus.

But the solution exists, and it's simple. In fact, it's in your hands. Because **you have the power to choose how you deal with stress** in challenging moments.

And this goes beyond flying, boo. It's important to apply these in your daily life as well. You can either let all that stress ruin your day and defeat you, or you can stay calm for a tiny fraction of a moment and let the storm pass.

The thing is that uncontrolled anger can be harmful to you and everyone around you. I know you cannot show your anger while working, but sometimes you'll be cornered that even the slightest sound, smell or a frown will push you over the edge. Let's talk about sensory overload. When your brain cannot organize and process all the different senses you're experiencing, you may feel agitated and triggered to react. This is common after a long, tiresome day when you feel irritable and restless to smell, touch, light, or sound. And it doesn't always have to be a great noise. You could be sitting at home, reading a book, when someone starts putting the dishes away. To make matters worse, thoughts and feelings can cause sensory overload, too. If there are too many at once, you may become agitated and even angry if you don't know how to process them.

Always ask yourself, **is it necessary for me to get upset?** Is this situation life-threatening? **Will my mind, in this state of anger, solve the problem I am facing?**

You'll find that almost always the answer is **NO.**

The BPTR technique is what I came up with, out of necessity many years ago, when I realized I was tired of living my life in a reactive mode.

BPTR stands for **Breathe-Pause-Think-Respond.** It's a simple technique that requires you to be fully conscious of what you are doing. And when you are conscious and fully present in your life, you're in control and have the power to respond instead of react.

Breathe. When something unexpected happens, just breathe. Take a deep breath in and exhale slowly.

Pause. Pause for a moment. Distract yourself with something, look through your purse or tie your shoe. Yawn. This distraction takes your mind off of the problem for a moment.

Think. Think of what you can do or say to make the situation better.

Ask yourself: Is it really necessary for me to get frustrated? **Am I in danger?**

Will my negative reaction solve the problem? NO.

Respond. This is the part that sets you free and makes your whole perspective on life different. If you follow the previous three steps correctly, this will be the easiest and most natural step in the process.

It doesn't take a long time for you to get back to your pre-anger state. Give yourself those ten seconds and do these steps in that time. If it helps, you can also count in your head, in the language of your choice. I know this works for me, especially when I start counting in Japanese.

I used to **react** to stressful moments in my life before. I still do sometimes, but now I am fully aware of my reaction. When I learned how to **respond** to stressful situations, I learned that the power to control myself is in me. When you react, you're defeated. You allow the other person to have power over you.

When you respond, you're in control. YOU are in charge.

16

No Is a Full Sentence

IF IT'S NOT A HELL YES, IT'S A NO

Saying no could be the ultimate self-care.
Claudia Black

Ma belle,

Have you ever been in a situation where you didn't have the courage to say no to the other person because you didn't want to disappoint them? Still, you felt frustrated with yourself for not being bold enough to act exactly how you felt at that moment.

I'm sure you have. And not just once, but many times. So why do we feel **obligated to say yes when we mean no?** What makes us change our minds even when we promise ourselves that we wouldn't do it again?

When I was a child, I remember my parents telling me never to accept gifts from strangers and to always say no if anyone offered to walk me home. This NO was embedded in my mind, and I knew that this was the only answer I would give, which kept me out of possible dangerous situations. Later on, as I developed some of my insecurities, saying no became one of the hardest things for me to do. By constantly being available to others, I was seeking their approval, trying to prove that I was worthy of their attention.

But that's not all. I wasn't only wasting my time on people who didn't deserve my attention, but I also found myself in situations where I couldn't say no anymore. On many occasions, I'd find myself doing flights on my days off when I really wanted to rest, or immediately changing my schedule to accommodate others without even thinking. This went on for years, and it also started influencing my relationships.

This is when I realized I was no longer myself. The only way out was to practice being bold, learn to love *me*, and put myself as a priority. I learned that there are ways you can say no politely and still not feel guilty. When you **don't explain yourself**, you actually appear much bolder in other people's eyes, **no matter how insecure you may feel at that moment.**

For example, when someone asks you for a favor you don't want to do, say no. If you end up disappointing that person, then that's for them to deal with. You were honest with them, but most importantly, you were **honest with yourself.** I know it's easier said than done, but there are ways to do it, and I know they work.

Saying no is not a bad thing. It just means that you have boundaries you respect.

Skybabe, **you do not have to justify yourself or find a reason you don't want to do something.**

Here's what I mean.

Don't Try to Fill the (Uncomfortable) Silence

When you talk to someone you feel uncomfortable with, they give you a choice and then wait for you to make a decision. You feel pressured to react as soon as possible, so you start talking, explaining yourself, and in the end, you end up saying yes to something you never wanted to do in the first place.

Remember that you do not have to say anything straight away. Just breathe, smile, and stay silent. Especially if you're on the phone. They can't see you! I guarantee you that the other person will start feeling uncomfortable. You're not obliged to say yes to anything if it doesn't feel right or light you up.

Start with *One* Clear NO

As simple as that. The more you practice, the easier it becomes. Be honest with yourself and **communicate** exactly **how you feel.** Be firm but polite. Of course, not all situations will be easy to handle. However, in most cases, if you are assertive but respectful, you'll do well. And this shouldn't be that difficult, *Skybabe*.

After all, we do this for a living.

Before you answer, think about what you want. If your gut tells you it's a definite no, say it and stay with your decision. Don't give a vague answer that will put you in a more difficult situation, especially if you're trying to avoid hurting that other person's feelings. This will only raise false hopes, leaving you with a preoccupied mind. Answering with a firm reply shows you are decisive, considerate toward the other person and have full respect for your time.

Understand the Other Person's Behavior

Some people would do anything to get you to say yes. Many would even go to that extent to bully you by becoming aggressive, forcing you into something you would never accept otherwise. Choose to stay calm and refuse to react to their aggressive behavior. You do not have to agree to anything. On the other hand, some people may try to make you feel guilty for not helping them out. Don't fall for this emotional blackmail. Think of all the times you've helped that person and never asked for anything in return. And of course, beware of the ones who will try to compliment you so that you feel obliged to accept their offer just because it sounds flattering. Uh-uh. Nope.

Know Your Worth

You are under no obligation to do anything you don't want to, *Skybabe*. Be self-ish. You are the most important person in your life, and you have every right to put your needs first. When you start prioritizing, you realize no one comes before you. So, if you don't feel like doing a favor to someone and you want to do your own thing, state it.

And as the amazing Lisa Nichols says, "Your job is to fill your own cup, so it overflows. Then you can serve others, joyfully, from your saucer."

Whenever you want to say no to something because you have more important things to do that are meaningful to you, remember to stay firm with your decision. You do not need to give a reason why you're saying no. Giving excuses and justifying yourself is unnecessary and unhelpful. **Stay true to yourself.**

Skybabe, have a look at these questions:

- **What am I saying YES to that I know I want to say NO to?**

- **What am I saying NO to that I know I want to say YES to?**

17

Get Out of Your Own Way

LEARN TO TRUST YOURSELF

*Self-sabotage is the smartest thing you can do if
you're sabotaging a self that is not really you.*
Armand Dimele

Habibti,

How many times have you sabotaged yourself only because
you persuaded yourself that you weren't worthy of the situation
you were in? And how many times have you dreamed of doing
something you've always wanted, but never dared to do anything
about it because you predicted you would fail?

I've been there, too.

Rarely able to say no to others, I constantly criticized my actions,
overanalyzing every word and situation. I became a professional
people pleaser, trapped in the vicious cycle of frustration, depres-
sion, and anger. And all because I thought I wasn't good enough.
I believed everyone else was more important than me and that
being imperfect meant being unsuccessful and undesirable.

I was sabotaging myself for years without even noticing. Without letting myself reflect on my decisions and learn from my mistakes.

Isn't this crazy, *Skybabe*? When you carry guilt deep in your heart, you feel you should be punished. Just think about it. When others don't show you the love you deserve, you have this uncontrollable need to be perfect and prove yourself. And because you feel unworthy and ashamed, you feel you need to compare yourself to others just to be accepted and appreciated.

So, how do you eliminate self-sabotage from your life and stop it from ruining every extraordinary trait you have?

By getting out of your own way.

And the only way to do it is to accept yourself with all your imperfections, while allowing yourself to see the real you. The magical YOU that needs help, love, and understanding only YOU can give.

When you feel broken, instead of feeling the need to appear whole and strong, allow yourself some time to become aware of your emotions. I know how hard it is when the feelings of guilt, blame, and shame after going against yourself for years never seem to fade. When they keep coming back, turning into insidious habits, leaving your brilliant but frightened mind paralyzed by limiting beliefs, perfectionism, and unrealistic expectations. When it becomes so familiar that you let it interfere with your life, and overtake your control like a chronic disease.

And this is especially true when things start going well in your life—when you get used to a certain level of comfort with yourself, in your relationships, and work. Anything new and better that pushes you past that comfort level signals your mind that you need to go back to where you were. That you are not good enough. That you are not worthy.

When this happens, it's time to take a step back to reflect on the situation and wholeheartedly accept everything good that is coming your way.

Embrace the discomfort.

It may seem difficult now, but soon enough, that same level of discomfort will become your new comfort zone. And as you embrace each step toward a better life and better you, you slowly push away all the limiting thoughts and beliefs.

You have every right to be proud of who you are; to stop feeling ashamed of how others see you and what they think of you.

It's time to stop sabotaging yourself.

I know it's impossible to make that change happen in an instant, but I also know that it's entirely possible to make a conscious decision to start working on your relationship with yourself, *Skybabe*.

To **forgive yourself.** To show yourself love and compassion.

You are ALWAYS one decision away from a completely different life, boo. Don't ever forget that. You can get to where you want to go when you make a conscious decision to take your life into your **own** hands and selfishly move toward your dream life.

So, the next time you feel you're ignoring your intuition, stop and think. Place your hand on your heart, and with a big smile on your face, say, **"I trust you."**

When you find yourself surrounded by the negativity that is draining your energy, leave. Find a nice, quiet place, and spend that time in silence, writing and reading, or do something that fills your soul with happiness.

When you start working on a new life-improving project, and fear of failure preoccupies your mind, take a step back. Remember the last time you wanted to quit but didn't? How amazing did you feel when you accomplished what you started?

When you overthink and worry about the things you cannot change, turn back and wave at your past. Know that it's never coming back and that it can never hurt you. Now look forward and embrace your future with a big smile.

You will emerge.

You will succeed because you are a winner, not a victim. And there is nothing in this world that can stop you, *Skybabe*.

SELF-NOURISHMENT

Being me-sponsible. My health, happiness, and well-being are in my hands.

18

If Your Body Could Talk, What Would It Say?

A TEMPLE WORTH FIGHTING FOR

Treat your body like it belongs to someone you love.
Unknown

Hey cuppy cake,

Are you enjoying the book? How is your flight going so far? Did you enjoy your food? You hear some kids screaming? A couple, three rows down, is drinking and laughing? Finding it hard to keep your focus? Put on your headphones or earplugs and tune out. I bet you'll love this one.

As women, we tend to take pretty good care of ourselves. Most of us have our favorite nail spas, hairstylists, and clothing brands. Our overall appearance is important, and we put great emphasis on our grooming. But when it comes to our bodies, there is always one feature we're not happy about—one tiny imperfection we believe we cannot change that makes us compare ourselves to other women who, to us, look better and fitter.

Skybabe, have you ever felt unworthy or undeserving because you thought you had flabby thighs, saggy breasts or stretch marks? Or that your fingers are too bony, face too round, and feet too wide?

I have, many times, and I am sure you have, too.

This makes me wonder, **whose standards do we live by?**

Should we care about what others think of how we look, or should we start focusing on ourselves and accept our bodies as they are?

A few years ago, while I was traveling through Italy, I had a chance to walk the streets of my childhood. I visited secret hideaways and remembered how wonderful it was to be a kid again. I remembered how much I enjoyed observing and admiring gracious and elegant Italian women walking the streets of Venice, Trieste, Milan, and Rome. The women that reminded me of the famous Sophia Loren, Gina Lollobrigida, and Claudia Cardinale, whose movies I loved to watch with my mom on early Sunday afternoons.

These incredible ladies will forever remain a symbol of femininity and women's empowerment, showing that beauty and grace go hand in hand with strength, courage, and perseverance.

Mesmerized by their confidence and gracefulness, I had always hoped to have the same attitude and affection toward myself. But as I grew up, I realized how easy it is to fall prey to society's expectations and critique. At school, I tried hard to cover the body parts I hated so that my peers wouldn't ridicule me. And every time someone commented on my weight or overall appearance, I'd defend myself. I'd say petty little stories that accentuated my flaws even more, as if I were sorry for the way I looked so that I wouldn't hurt the other person's feelings.

This only injected fear and self-doubt into my already weakened self-esteem. I got into the trap of caring how others saw my body and let the thoughts of despair overpower me. But as I matured and my priorities changed, I decided not to let anyone destroy the most important relationship I'd ever have—the relationship with myself.

I knew I didn't want to change the attributes that meant nothing to others, but everything to me. So, I started working on becoming the best version of myself. When I began to look at things from a slightly different perspective, I discovered how easy it is to fall in love with yourself. I focused on what I have instead of what I don't have. I learned that working hard on your body and appearance has nothing to do with how much makeup you put on or how often you visit your hairdresser or manicurist. It has everything to do with how you see and treat yourself. With how much love and compassion you're willing to show to your body and how determined you are to make it healthier and better.

This was especially true during my flying years. I can't tell you how many times a passenger or a colleague commented on my looks. Even if they were complimenting me, their opinion shouldn't have been important to me. But when I was in uniform, I knew I was safe. We all looked pretty similar, and it felt good to hide behind that non-waisted jacket and a slightly looser skirt.

I tried so many procedures to make my skin look perfect. I even completed ten sessions of LPG cellulite treatment, thinking that once I was finished, my legs would finally be cellulite free. In theory, this is what was supposed to happen and what the dermatologist promised. In reality, Mother Nature had different lessons she wanted to teach me.

While I lost inches around my thighs and waist and saw an immediate improvement in my skin tone and elasticity, once the treatment was over, the cellulite came back and my skin was nowhere near as smooth and sexy as I thought it would be. Still, I was grateful for the experience, but I was mad at myself for once again searching for the magic pill that would make everything perfect.

That magic pill and magic wand do not exist, *Skybabe*. Your determination and love toward yourself do. And this is the only way to get the body you want and improve your overall health.

It took years for me to become the woman who is comfortable in her skin. And with life's new challenges, I still struggle sometimes. But I'm more mindful nowadays because I know that **accepting your body is a start, loving it is progress, but teaching your mind to respect it is a sure path to a lasting change.**

We're all a work in progress, *Skybabe,* and we need to give ourselves **time to evolve.**

Now, pause for a moment and think. When was the last time you massaged your feet, or hugged yourself? I know it's easy to get that much-needed full body massage on layovers but, how often do you look in the mirror and smile at what you see?

Your incredible body is undeniably beautiful when you stop looking for flaws. Give it attention and love, embrace it, and love it selflessly because it has always been there for you. It has helped you and carried you all your life.

Thank your feet for taking you places and allowing you to explore the world. Thank your creative hands for making beautiful masterpieces and your strong stomach for digesting all the junk food you've ever eaten. Love your eyes no matter what color they are.

Be happy with being *you*. Start working on getting fitter and healthier. Exercising regularly doesn't have to be a chore. It can be as enjoyable as any other daily activity, as long as you give it priority and understand how important it is. Your daily habits determine how your future unfolds, and you have the power to make a decision right now.

The next time you start obsessing about cellulite and stretch marks before putting your bikini on, remember how good your body is to you. No matter what you think of it, your body never lets you down. Practice being kind to it, protect it with all your might, and don't let anyone speak ill of it. Ever. Because it's your only home.

Your body loves you.

It's time to give some love back and fall in love with taking care of yourself. Remember, self-confidence starts with self-love.

What is one small change you can make today to start feeling the way you want to feel about yourself?

Now, tune in and answer the following questions:

- **What does self-love mean to you?**

- **How would you rate your self-love on a scale from 1 to 10?**

- **When you feel a craving coming, what do you do? Do you immediately satisfy your hunger, distract yourself, or become aware of these feelings?**

- **What do you love about your body?**

- **What do you hate about it?**

- **How often do you make time to exercise, practice self-care, and do the things you love?**

- **Why and when do you make compromises?**

Now, imagine you had **the power to speak to the little 7-year-old girl in you.** Write a letter to her. **What would you tell her?**

19

Eat to Live or Live to Eat

THE PERFECT DIET . . . OR WHY DIETS DON'T WORK

> Given half the chance, the human body will heal
> itself by itself.
> *Joshua Rosenthal*

Hey *bella,*

Did you get a chance to stretch your legs and get some piping-hot water from the galley for your tea? Now that you're cozy and warm, all snuggled up in that seat, let's move on. Shall we?

I don't remember if I came back from Cuba, Puerto Rico or Jamaica then, but I know this was the flight I had on my roster following my Caribbean-style vacation in one of those gorgeous, exotic places. I simply adore the ocean, sea, and the islands. What I also love is to explore the food of the places I travel to. I really enjoy it and eat with no restrictions. Any. Really.

As you very well know, operating that first flight after any vacation gives you wings. Feeling fresh and doing everything with ease, you have more energy than your colleagues, and you're excited to be there. You simply radiate. And this is exactly how I felt.

Besides being so thrilled to be back, knowing that I was going to Bangkok made all the difference. Like I didn't have enough on my vacation, I was already planning to eat more. In my mind, I had already pictured the sweetest mouth-watering mangoes in the whole wide world. I was hoping to get a good massage, have nice food, and do some shopping, too.

Life was good.

And ... my skirt was tight. Like, really nicely sexy tight. *Damn.*

With my bum sticking out and my curves showing, I felt good. And I thought my uniform finally fit me the way I wanted. In most companies, there would have been nothing wrong with the way I looked.

But not in mine. No, mama!

The skirt I had on was already run-down and due for replacement. It shrank over time, but now coming back from a vacation where I pampered myself with all kinds of delicious food and more than likely gained an extra kilo or two, the skirt was tight and calling for attention. *Honk! Hooooonk!*

I realized this once it was too late, so I just hoped my senior wouldn't notice and tell me off for it. And I was still high from the good times I had on my vacation, that honestly, I didn't actually care much what anyone would say.

I kept munching my way through Bangkok, indulging in Pad Thai, mango sticky rice, and loads of coconut water. And as a finisher, coming back from Bangkok, I visited three of my favorite sweet biscuit stands at the airport itself, where they always served free samples. I would happily pass by all of them any time I was operating a Bangkok flight. And since they were conveniently spread out on my long way to the gate, I knew strategically how to organize myself and take a little bit from each. I would buy some boxes, too. I promise.

This time was no exception, but I also talked so much about it to other colleagues that I ended up with three of them following me to the stands.

And then, in a split second, as I turned to check on my colleagues, I saw the Purser. I knew I wasn't doing anything wrong, but her disapproving eyes told me I was next on her list. Until that time, I was already working as a senior for a few years, so I was in charge of the team of eight people, including the three girls I was strolling along with. With that in mind, I should have been a role model. Not someone who talks other *Skybabes* into stuffing their faces with yummy biscuits on their way to the gate. That was the company's policy, but honestly, I didn't give a damn about it on that day. My tush in a tight skirt craved those small, crunchy, chocolate-coated biscuits, and all I cared about was getting one.

Funnily enough, I didn't even eat processed sweets, but at the time, it was a cute, playful, and fun thing to do. The four of us strolled happily along the terminal, laughing and munching on delicious treats, after which we got to the gate on time. Just as good students at school would do.

Everything went well until I got a call from the Purser somewhere toward the end of the flight. She asked me to come to the First Class galley for a quick chat. Don't you just hate those, *Skybabe*?

I knew she was going to preach about company standards and regulations. I wasn't supposed to eat in uniform, ESPECIALLY not as a senior. But knowing that I had an immaculate file, amazing reports from seniors, colleagues, and passengers, I wasn't afraid that she'd question the quality of my work or level of performance. I knew my cheeky biscuits were to blame.

So, I stuck my neck out and listened. I sat across from the Purser waiting for her to tell me off, like a kid in front of a teacher in kindergarten. After a short, meaningless chit-chat, to ease me into the conversation, I was pretty sure she didn't fancy me at all. While I was still cheerful and professional, her heavy voice told me a different story. Like a volcano waiting to erupt, she stared at me with prying eyes, scrutinizing my every move. Just as I'd predicted, a lava of colorful words came out of her mouth, disregarding everything I had done well on the flight. But one sentence struck me so much that after it, I didn't even bother focusing on the rest of her gibberish.

"Have you considered going on a DIET?"

I couldn't help but chuckle at her abrupt question. *Did she just say diet?* When I saw how astonished she was by my instinctive reaction, I paused, trying to swallow a lump in my throat. Her blabbering continued for a few moments, but only one word kept ringing in my head. *Diet. Diet. Diet.*

My skirt was too tight, and I needed to lose weight. Goodness. I looked at her, then I looked at my belly. Then again at her, then again at my belly. Sure, I was slightly bloated, but who isn't during the flight? And yes, my skirt should have been looser by the company standards, but it fit me perfectly. Then, of course, she added I was a terrible example of a leader for luring my crew members into snacking at the airport.

To get her to stop talking, I nodded and stood up.

I know, I know, I shouldn't have allowed her to lower my vibe just like that, but her points made me wonder. I was an active health and fitness coach and Zumba instructor who worked her butt off on the ground when she wasn't flying. I took pride in teaching healthy lifestyle habits, helping my clients get fitter and healthier, attending classes around the world, and getting licensed in various disciplines. I knew the struggles *Skybabes* faced with food, exercise, and weight loss. And here, somebody was telling *me* I needed to go on a diet. The one thing I never believed in.

The Purser knew nothing about me. I was just a number in uniform to her; another senior colleague. But she was a typical example of someone who thinks that diets can change it all. A magic cloth to sweep off your weight problems like dust over a piece of furniture and *voilà,* there you go. Suddenly, you're a shiny, sexy Barbie doll without a single problem in life.

Diets simply don't work.

Because **there is no one-size-fits-all diet.** What works for one person doesn't guarantee success for the other.

So, shall we get a bit deeper into it?

Diets are a gigantic topic, and it's practically impossible to include all the facts, recommendations, as well as past and current trends in one place. And I'm not here to preach or scold. I simply want to help you think of how **you can improve your relationship with food.** Because your relationship with food is much more than shoving a spoon or a fork into your mouth to feed yourself to survive.

It is the mirror of how you live your life and what is going on in it.

My personal story and interest in diets, food, and health began years ago, when I was in high school. I didn't live in a family that had the abundance of . . . well, anything. Food included. There was always something on the table to eat, but that something wasn't necessarily what I liked. I craved packed sugary fruit juices. My eyes were hungry for sweets, more meat and fruit. I underestimated the efforts my mom made while preparing everything from scratch, often using our own produce from our garden.

As a little girl, I used to spend weekends in the countryside, playing in nature, taking care of chickens and doing all kinds of farm work. Collecting eggs when hens laid them and climbing cherry trees while devouring the sweetest and juiciest cherries by the mouthful were some of my favorite things to do. I loved picking grapes from the swirling wines that my dad so diligently took care of every day. Of course, there were things I dreaded, like collecting ripe plums for jam preparation or weeding out spring onions.

While these memories are so dear to my heart now, I feel sorry for not having been able to notice and appreciate the wealth of health we had then. All the fresh produce we ate was local and organic. My mum and dad worked hard to grow all that wonderful food, and my sister and I worked alongside them.

Only now, when I know so much more about the food industry and unreasonably high organic food prices, I can see the true value and the quality of the food I grew up eating.

During high school, I remember being sick for most of one school year. I would visit the doctor every single month because I had stubborn flu symptoms that wouldn't go away. From month to month, the doctor would prescribe antibiotics and I blindly followed his advice, as many of us do.

After at least seven rounds of antibiotics, in less than a year, I didn't get any better. Although I loved my doctor, because he was patient and kind, I started questioning his methods. How come he never asked about my eating and sleeping habits or my lifestyle?

Finally, I sat down and started connecting the dots, slowly realizing how important they all were to my overall health. I saw the big picture. While I don't remember my eating habits at the time and the cause of my sickness, I realize that this episode in my life planted a seed of curiosity toward a healthy lifestyle.

Food can be medicine. But it can be poison, too. Whatever you put in your body, your body feels and reacts to it.

I spent years of my life not seeing any connection between the food I mindlessly shoved into my body and the quality of life I led. How about the sleeping patterns and the way I lived daily?

These are some simple questions that weren't that obvious to me then. I lived on autopilot, treating my life as if I had seven more in my pocket. **I was oblivious to the fact that my body memorized everything I'd ever put in it and everything I ever said to it.** And right now, if you have a moment of guilt about the overload of tiramisu or chips you recently had on one of your trips, don't batter yourself over it. This wasn't my intention. Please know that things have an effect if they're regularly repeated, especially when they become part of your habitual behavior, not as a one-time event.

And you know what's amazing? Your body is such a perfect human machine that is made to regenerate and rebuild itself—your blood cells, your organs, the whole of you. But you have to allow it to do the work by choosing the right food in order to help it stay healthy. **Be patient with it. Love it. Cherish every part of your body.**

Fast forward to the time I became *Skybabe*, I dove deeper into the world of fitness. I also became more interested in health and the role of food in my life. Soon after I started training more consistently and working with my clients, I realized that the game changer was not how often or how much I exercised. It was the food I ate. So, I wanted to know more.

I finished a year-long course and became a certified Integrative Nutrition Health Coach (Institute for Integrative Nutrition, NY). It was the best decision I ever made. I learned so much and changed many of my lifestyle habits for the better. The school opened the door to a whole new world of wellness with a holistic approach that spoke to me on so many levels.

Although my school presents and integrates over 100 dietary theories into its curriculum, it doesn't recommend any specific diet. We follow what we call the principle of **bio-individuality.**

What does that actually mean?

Everyone is different. You are a completely unique bio-individual shaped by your heritage, age, race, gender, culture, height, weight, blood type, activity level, lifestyle, geographical location, etc. The person you are now is not the same person you were in the past, or the person you will be in the future. **As you evolve, your dietary needs change with time.** Bio-individuality puts individuals before any diet or theory. It also classifies food into two groups: primary and secondary.

Primary food is the food that is not served on a plate, but still nourishes us: relationships, spirituality, career, and physical activity—the main pillars to achieving superior health. They are, in fact, the ones that determine how we eat the food that goes through our mouth, which is called **secondary food.**

The quality of the secondary food is affected by the quality of the primary food.

Allow me to explain.

It might not seem so obvious, but try to think of a day when you felt emotionally unfulfilled, sad, angry or fatigued. How did you eat then? Did you crave sugar, alcohol, cigarettes more? Maybe fried food? Did you finish that chocolate, a can of Coke or a bottle wine without even noticing?

It's almost as if, by satisfying our cravings, we get an instant solution to the problems we face. A feel-good sensation. But, the one that lasts a moment and then backfires.

I find it hard to forget all those days and nights when I would come home from flights at odd hours. As the passengers disembarked, I was there, barely standing on my two feet, wanting to disappear.

Now, I am in a taxi, after an eventful long-haul flight, absorbing the driver's endless questions about how often I travel to his home country. Lord, have mercy! I can barely talk. My eyelids are closing like Tom Cat's. *Can you, please, just stop talking and let me enjoy the silence?*

Look, I've always been a kind and enthusiastic chatterbox, but in those phases of fatigue, from time to time, I looked more like a fire-spitting dragon ready to devour the taxi driver's head.

Moving on, I look forward to the warm shower and the mild scent of my favorite soap and shampoo scrubbing off the dirt. I get home and put all the groceries I bought on the trip in the fridge. Familiar?

But, hmm, hey, you! Yes, you! Chocolate. Let me open you, you irresistible little bastard. I'll just have one piece, maybe two, and then I'll put you back in the freezer. I promise. As far away as possible. Out of my mind. But then, one piece becomes two and soon I devour the entire bar in less than ten minutes. Especially if it's the luxuriously soft and creamy ROYCE' chocolate you just brought from Japan.

Oh, well! What do I do now?

I'll go take a shower and try to sleep for a few hours. Yes, that's it. Mind the sugar rush and the disturbed quality of sleep.

I wake up feeling broken and tired. It's late afternoon. "Normal" people are slowly winding down, finishing their working day, and where am I?

In a vacuum. Somewhere undefined. Where days of the week don't matter. The only thing that does is where you fly to and what time you get up to go to work.

I drag myself to the kitchen and open the fridge. I stand there looking and searching for something to eat and after some time, I take out bread and butter. Mmm, nice. I'll toast the bread and melt some butter on top. What a nutritious lunch, right? My (fat) ass!

Skybabe, let's be honest here. Brutally honest. When you feel this fatigued, what cravings do you have? Chips with a creamy mayonnaise dip? Copious amounts of coffee that make your heart want to jump out of your chest? Or a whole packet of gummy bears?

Whatever it is, I'm sure you recognize yourself in these lines and understand the point of how and when cravings occur. The fact is that how you feel affects how you eat. Period.

So, how do we fix this?

If you are a regular human, or should I rather specify and say—if you belong to our fantastic line of *Skybabes*—the chances of you experimenting with diets in your flying career are huge.

Whereas some diets may work for you and some may not, we believe that following the 80/20 rule covers it all: strive to eat healthy 80 percent of the time and the remaining 20 eat joyfully and guilt-free. This is sustainable and brings long-lasting results.

Now, let's go back to that infamous travel bloat from the beginning of the book.

FART ALERT (OTHERWISE KNOWN AS THE TRAVEL BLOAT)

Travel bloat is incredibly common and can also be amazingly annoying and painful, so let's see some causes, i.e. foods that can provoke it, other than the pressure itself, as we've already seen it. There will also be some suggestions on how to avoid it successfully because we want the fresh smell of violets and roses from our bloating tummies! Oh, yeah!

We did the research and took our invaluable experience into account. We talked to *Skybabes* and frequent travelers. We also contacted a few doctors of aviation and travel medicine. Here is what we came to know.

As always, flight attendants have their own expressions for this flying phenomenon. Some refer to their heavy bloated stomach as a "jet belly."

Out of all travel challenges, this one stinks most.

So what can you do about feeling gassy and bloated while flying?

Drink water regularly.

Definitely the best and number one thing you can do for your tummy. Not only will it keep you hydrated, but it can really lessen the bloating and hence farting. My suggestion is to have your own reusable water bottle that you can easily refill throughout the flight. Yes, you might go to the lavatory much more frequently, but compared to the downsides of not having enough of it, it's surely worthy of your frequent loo visits if Mother Nature calls. To add one more important thing—do not wait for too long to pee, and never postpone or hold it.

On busy flights with rivers of passengers, remember that you, too, are a human with needs, just like everybody else. Just go.

It's a priority! I'm saying this as a guilty-as-charged-professional-pee-holder and someone who time and time again neglected herself, which was never a good idea!

Do not repeat my mistakes, *Skybabe!*

Stay away from fizzy drinks.

Since bubbles expand in your stomach, they could further the feelings of bloat, especially in the air. They are also always full of sugar, so yes, skip them! And if you are wondering if diet/light versions of soda drinks are a better option, skip them, too! Artificial sweeteners are even worse for your body than pure sugar. They might have fewer calories, but they can be very addictive and have no nutritional value.

Watch your caffeine intake.

In today's world, where coffee has become synonymous with staying awake, it's worth to take a different stance and give it all a thought. While no one denies it is a delicious drink, coffee can affect each of us in different ways, but what is sure is that it can dehydrate you and that, too, can lead to bloating. Taking dairy milk with it worsens the feeling, but more on that later in a few lines.

Do not take too much orange juice, although "freshly" squeezed.

Contrary to popular belief, orange juice isn't all that healthy. Not only does it have an extremely high percentage of sugar, which is not healthy ground or sky, it can also affect bloating. I remember one captain telling me this "in-flight secret" a long time ago and since I stopped having it and started observing my digestion more, I noticed he was right. Aside from getting the knowledge from books or online, experiment with yourself and learn what works for you.

Avoid gassy foods, such as beans and lentils.

Rinsing, soaking, and sprouting the beans or lentils is a good way to reduce bloating. Changing the soaking water several times before the actual cooking can also help. This, of course, refers to preparing and eating food before the flight.

What to eat instead: Some beans are easier on the digestive system. Pinto beans and black beans may be more digestible, especially after soaking. You can also replace beans with grains and quinoa. Light-colored lentils are generally lower in fiber than darker ones, and may therefore cause less bloating, too.

Avoid broccoli and other cruciferous vegetables.

Cooking cruciferous vegetables (cauliflower, broccoli, cabbage, Brussels sprouts) makes them easier to digest. If you're wondering what to eat instead, know that there are many alternatives, including spinach, cucumbers, lettuce, sweet potatoes, and zucchini. This also goes for onion and garlic, especially raw.

Avoid dairy products, such as milk, cheese, yogurt, and butter.

I agree this one is difficult to resist, but did you know that about 75 percent of the world's population can't break down lactose, the sugar found in milk? This condition is known as lactose intolerance. If you're lactose intolerant, dairy products can cause major digestive problems for you. Symptoms include bloating, gas, cramping, and diarrhea.

What to eat instead: People who are lactose intolerant can sometimes handle cream and butter, or fermented dairy like yogurt. Lactose-free and dairy-free products are also available, like coconut, almond, oat, soy, quinoa, rice milk and yogurt. Alternatives are always available. Look for them, try them, and see what works for you.

Walk around the plane frequently to "shake up your bowels."

Flight attendants are moving a lot in the cabin and that is how it should be, for many reasons. For a while, I was flying and counting the number of steps on the device attached to my skirt way before fancy fitness trackers became a thing. Although I knew I was extremely active, even compared to my other colleagues, I had no clue that walking up and down the tube for 7 hours was enough for me to make around 12,000-13,000 steps. Fun but true. That was a LOT! And it surely helped me with shaking my bowels.

When it comes to releasing the air, remember that farts are essentially a cocktail of various gases. Only a tiny portion of that actually smells. When our body naturally wants to push something out and we consciously won't allow it, it's not like all that flatulence disappears. Instead, it can lead to discomfort, pain, more bloating, and other health issues.

To sum up: Let your farts fly when you do, and ROCK ON!

THE WATER BOTTLE TRICK

Airplane cabins are pressurized at somewhere between 6,000 and 8,000 feet, which is a significant altitude change for your body if you've come from sea level. And just as the air in your water bottle expands at higher altitudes, the gas in your intestines can expand on the plane, growing to take up about 30 percent more room than usual. Then it needs to escape. *Mamma mia!*

But where?!

To be sure we are on the same page, here is a brief explanation and an example of the plastic water bottle phenomenon. Remember, you can try this yourself and experiment with it.

The next time you operate a flight or travel as a passenger, take any pet plastic water bottle available on board. Before takeoff, have at least a glass for yourself from that same bottle, so you don't leave it full.

In any case, *Skybabes* always need water after an active and efficient boarding, to begin with. Often we even break a sweat with all the passengers' luggage locomotion in the cabin.

Next, close the cap tightly and place the bottle in a secure stowage before getting ready for departure. Then, after takeoff and when the seatbelt sign is off, get up from your jumpseat, and go directly to your bottle. Notice how it looks. Has something changed? Is it pumped with pressure? Does it look airtight? Now, try to open it quickly! More often than not, water will splash you in the face and it will almost look as if you were opening a soda drink after shaking it. Right?

Then, as the flight progresses and you're slowly sipping your water, keep observing if the bottle shape changes.

But hang on a minute. The best and the most interesting part hasn't come just yet—descent time. Once the aircraft starts descending, go check your bottle. Notice how it slowly starts shrinking and deforming?

And the result comes just after landing. Seriously, is this weird twisted plastic thing the same bottle you drank from? It doesn't look like it at all.

The truth is that you must have seen this happen on flights time and time again, but maybe you paid little attention to it or just didn't notice the connection between your own body, especially your tummy, and the pressure. The same thing happens to your blood vessels. As most of your body is made of water, you can let your imagination loose and picture multiple bottles inside of you, pumping in and out.

So now that you are completely aware of this, add bloating and farting as a cherry on the top and the actual party begins!

20

The Very Hungry Caterpillar Meets the Greedy Pelican

A BAD CASE OF SUGAR ADDICTION

All I really need is love, but a little chocolate now
and then doesn't hurt.
Lucy Van Pelt

Our award-winning chefs have prepared a treat for you today. From a cappuccino of wild mushrooms, parched hamour in citrus salsa, to coriander and bean ragout. The choice is yours. And for dessert, we proudly offer you a symphony of sweets: honey and chocolate cheesecake, mixed berry truffle, and a one-pound chocolate bar. Wait. *What?*

Ah, *Skybabe,*

You did it again. You stuffed yourself with all the food you could find, even though you promised you wouldn't overeat. In fact, you promised yourself that you would start exercising, eating well, and taking care of your body once and for all.

But you didn't.

I know the feeling, boo. I've been there, too.

I remember the day I locked myself in my apartment after a long-haul flight, exhausted and unhappy. After an entire week of flying, I finally got a well-deserved day off. And instead of spending that day sleeping, rejuvenating, and working on myself, all I wanted to do was cry.

Which I did.

Except, I didn't just cry.

I ate sugar—the magic cure for all my ailments that brought ultimate joy, instant satisfaction, and awful guilt and pity toward myself.

This had a major impact on my body and mind, and while I ran on the treadmill to keep the pounds off, my skin and teeth suffered from sensitivity, I felt lethargic and frustrated, and certainly didn't feel like doing anything. And I mean, *anything*.

Sometimes I'd eat fatty, sugary treats the entire flight, without giving myself a chance to eat a proper, nutritious meal.

But what is it that makes us binge on sweets, *Skybabe?* Do we purposely persuade ourselves that we're still hungry or is it because we think that once we eat the forbidden fruit, we might as well overeat, since we haven't been true to ourselves?

While science has an excellent explanation for this, I won't get into detail here. I'll leave that research to you. But what I will do is show you exactly what I did to get out of this endless cycle.

Over the years, I've had enough episodes of binge eating, especially chocolate. Imagine eating 3-4 Snickers bars in a day just so you could keep moving and working without having to stop and take a proper lunch break.

So wrong, I know!

But no decadent indulgence was worth my suffering. I was sick of getting sick, hating myself and my lack of will to do something about my life. I was desperate for a change, and I was determined to make it happen.

After a few months, I decided to take action to curb my sugar cravings. I signed up for a wellness program that I'd been telling myself I would enroll in, but never had the courage to take the necessary steps.

Because I never knew I was addicted until I tried to stop.

I'll never forget the day I drove to the venue. Just reaching the place was an enormous success for me. But the moment I got there, I freaked out. Suddenly, the realization that I could no longer have sugar in my life when it was giving me so much comfort slapped me on my face and I nearly lost it. I wasn't ready to quit. All I could think of was getting one more bite of my favorite chocolate bar while promising myself, "I'm quitting tomorrow."

Unable to catch my breath, all I wanted to do was to bolt out of there and never return. Naturally, after a week of not having sweets, I dreamed of running to the nearest store and stuffing myself with every kind of candy bar I could think of.

But I didn't.

After days of crying in agony and successfully completing the workshop, I continued without sugar for the entire month. I promised myself that I would let go of the one thing that was making me happy momentarily but holding me back in so many areas of my life.

And that's when something incredible happened. I noticed that the more I held off sugar, the more I pushed myself to pursue other things. All of a sudden, I started making better food choices. I didn't want to eat junk that I actually hated, but chose to eat because it was a simpler and easier option. Postponing the immediate gratification and choosing not to eat what was actually hurting me made me a much happier, more productive person.

If you've tried everything and still can't curb your cravings no matter how hard you try, check out these five simple steps that may make a huge difference in your life, *Skybabe*. Whether you decide to do them all or just the ones that suit your needs, make sure you give them a try. The whole point is to pass beyond that moment of pleasure and satisfaction and realize that you don't need all that fat and sugar to feel happy and satisfied.

Be Prepared

When you plan your meals in advance, you know that your food is ready for you to eat and that you won't have the slightest chance of reaching for junk. This powerful habit changed the way I look at food today. It's important to start from somewhere so, do this at home on your day off.

Put all the food that you are going to eat for the day on the table. Take a good look at it. Feel it. Smell it. Divide it into three to five sections, three for main meals and two for snacks if you decide to have them. When you see your food in front of you, your brain actually acknowledges that there is enough food for you to eat and that you won't go hungry. Plus, you'll know exactly what you're putting in your body.

This is the number one step that made all the difference for me. I am a visual person and I like to plan. Even if you think you can't do this, just look at it this way: the effort you make in those 15 minutes a day when preparing and packing your meals for the following day cannot be compared to having to run around, searching for something to eat when you're already starving.

I started with raw food—mostly fruits, vegetables, nuts, seeds, and salads, so I could easily pack and munch on it while flying. I also made sure I took the time to eat my lunch, no matter how busy I was. And I know that timing your meals on board can be painfully difficult, but it's not impossible. It just takes some planning. Those 10-15 minutes you give yourself while eating will not only make you eat properly, but will also give you a much-needed moment to refresh your mind and stretch your body. It's true, some flights will be crazy busy, but you *must* find 10 minutes for yourself. If it's a quick turnaround and you cannot find the time, make sure you eat before you leave your house. Never go to work hungry. A lesson I learned the hard way.

Brush Your Teeth

When you can't stop thinking about eating that doughnut or chocolate bar, just go brush your teeth. Yes, even on board. And if you're worried about your makeup, stop! It'll take you less than a minute to reapply that lipstick.

That nice, squeaky clean sound your teeth make after you brush them will help. And the taste of minty toothpaste doesn't really go well with anything, so it sure will stop you from shoving anything in your mouth, at least for a while.

Gross Yourself Out

I know it sounds weird, but this one never fails. All you need to do is to watch a short video on what processed sugar does to your organs and after two minutes of watching, you'll forget about eating that fatty treat. And, good ole YouTube is loaded with videos that can help you.

When you know you have sugar cravings and find it hard to resist them, stop for a moment to think about what actually causes them. What makes you put toxins in your body that ultimately make you feel worse and guilty about indulging in those terrible, sugary treats?

Don't Buy Junk (Food)

Do not have anything in the house that you know isn't good for you. This is rule number one in my house and it works really well. Out of sight, out of mind. Over time, it will become a habit, and when you walk into a store and visit the candy aisle, you won't bat an eyelash. Or even better, you'll be skipping the candy aisle entirely.

Drink Water or a Cup of Herbal Tea

When you have your meals planned, there is a very slight chance that you'll be hungry between the meals, actually. So, most of the time, you may experience that feeling of reaching for a quick, unhealthy snack out of pure boredom. So instead, drink some water or a nice fresh cup of herbal tea.

Stay strong and know that you are not alone in this, Sugar boo. Take it from a former sugar addict who could eat a 400g *Toblerone* bar in a matter of minutes. Hard to believe? Well, imagine a pelican gulping the fish it just caught. Still not clear? How about a whale in migration, gliding through the ocean, with its mouth wide open? Still struggling to picture it? Okay, just think of a trash can. That's exactly what it was like. Dumping garbage into the body I should have treated with care.

It took me months and years to get to where I am today and come up with techniques that actually work. It took fake smiles, silent cries, and many tough decisions to realize that nothing can break me unless I allow it.

You are a warrior, *Skybabe,* and your body is a temple, so treat it with love and respect. When you feel frustrated, overwhelmed and close to giving up, just remember that you have the power within you to change how you feel. Make small daily steps and stay determined. Tell yourself that you love yourself more than sugar. Write little love notes to your body. Keep reminding yourself that you don't need sugar to feel satisfied. And don't forget to keep track of your progress. Use your journal to write about your successes and struggles.

Just after a few weeks of quitting sugar, you'll see incredible results. Be proud of yourself. Take a note of how far you've come.

And don't stop. It's a journey. So you might as well enjoy it.

21

You Slipped Up, Skybabe

WHEN HEALTHY IS TOO HEALTHY

To eat is a necessity, but to eat intelligently is an art.
François de la Rochefoucauld

"Okay, okay, I still have another half an hour before my wake-up call! I can make it! Yes, yes, yes! Let me check out this health food store and grab some stuff. Oh, God! Vienna has countless amazing and cheap-as-chips places for shopping! I'll quickly have one last peep!"

I glanced at my watch and rushed into the shop with a big smile on my face. There was an enormous selection of healthy foods and I wanted them ALL. My pupils dilated out of joy at seeing the beauty in front of me. Still, I had to remind myself that I was running out of time and couldn't do my usual aisle browsing, food label reading, and product tasting. Like car brakes squeaking to a full stop at the red traffic light, my eyes fixated on one item in particular.

Aronia! The Berry Queen!

"Oh, you, sweet superberrrry! Come over here!"

I snatched the 330mL bottle of concentrated Aronia juice, collected a few other items from the store, and paid before whizzing through the revolving door.

Now, before I move on, I have to throw light on one thing. I've always been a berry lover. I've adored berries my whole life. All kinds of them. During childhood, my parents would rarely buy them for my sister and me, so I could never get enough. Especially blueberries that had always been my favorite. But during this period, I was obsessed with another type of berry—Aronia (also called black chokeberry). I intensely read and researched its health benefits, but I couldn't easily get a hold of it. Hence, finally seeing it here, within my hand's reach, and at an affordable price, I did my Snoopy dance out of excitement, impatient to try it as soon as I could.

It was nearly time to prepare for the flight. While I didn't get enough rest, I knew the flight would be easy and quick, so I didn't worry too much. I put my uniform on, got myself ready for the flight, and opened the bottle of my sweet *berrylicious* nectar.

And then I took a sip.

Strong and tart, but *mmm* . . . I loved the taste. Although each time I swallowed, my mouth parched, Aronia was calling me for more.

Knowing all its health properties, I was convinced that it would do me good and enhance my energy for the work hours that followed. So, I kept having more. And more. And more. When I finished half, I took a break.

Then, in the middle of fixing my hair and putting my makeup on, it suddenly crossed my mind that I wouldn't be able to take this bottle with me. *Scheiße!*

I didn't want to risk putting it in the suitcase, either. *If that bottle opens, I'm screwed.* As well as all my clothes.

Well, what the heck. I am not throwing it for sure. So, I took another sip. And another. And another. Until I completely devoured it.

With each new gulp, I felt slightly more nauseous.

The TV changed its shape, and the paintings on the wall started spinning. Sweating profusely with shivers and nausea, I galloped to the bathroom, only to see my pale face in the mirror, which soon turned red and pale again.

Something wasn't right.

Then, with an unstoppable force, the deep red Iguazú Falls flew out of my mouth straight into the washbasin. I vomited all the Aronia I had in my tummy. Looking all chic and posh with a neat hairstyle and makeup on just two minutes ago, I turned into an instant berry porridge prepared hastily on the morning run to work.

To my surprise, after I threw up, my body quickly recovered. It took me a good few minutes to come to my senses and realize what had just happened. I fixed my makeup again, rearranged my hair, and stuffed the rest of my things into the suitcase. With heels on, bag on my shoulder and a picture-perfect smile, I was ready. My foot kick-pushed the door wide open and off I went. Just to act as if nothing had happened.

Unbelievable! I realized how my body rejected everything it didn't need and couldn't take in. It is so amazingly clever. It just knows. If only I had listened to it, instead of continuing with my stubborn drinking. That Aronia juice was a concentrate, and it was meant to be taken in small shots or diluted each day, not a whole frigging bottle at once!

What about spirulina, green tea, chia seeds, and all kinds of supplements? They all lived their popularity phases on board. Who else witnessed this? Raise your hand!

I'm sure you remember massively buying all the superfoods you could fit in your suitcase without knowing how much you need or what is good for you. While I'm not saying you shouldn't consume healthy food, especially superfoods, what I *am* saying is this: know what YOUR body needs. Read about it, do your research, consult a health coach, a nutritionist or talk to a doctor. And when you get the knowledge and enough info, decide what's best for you and your health. Healthy doesn't mean it's good specifically for you. As in my case, my healthy Aronia was way TOO healthy, and it made me sick. I had an overdose of health!

Get my point, *Skybabe?*

So, let's dive in and give you a brief introduction to SUPERFOODS that we think can help you while flying.

What are Superfoods and why are they called SUPERfoods?

Superfoods are a class of the most potent, super-concentrated, and nutrient-rich foods on the planet. Superfoods can increase the vital force and energy of one's body and are the optimum choice for improving overall health—boosting the immune system, elevating serotonin production, enhancing sexuality, lowering inflammation, and alkalizing the body. Wow, right? Give me some, you say! And I agree.

But, let's move on and see what superfoods are right for you, *Skybabe.*

Do an online research today and you'll see a different, maybe even longer list of superfoods. And that's okay. Because that means you're eager to learn more. You're taking your health into your own hands, questioning things! Kudos to you!

There are some researchers who even see onion as a superfood. And if onion is your superfood, go for it. I wouldn't include it in this list, but I completely agree that onion has some amazing health properties. So, **the choice is always yours.**

As superfoods are vibrant, nutritionally dense foods that offer tremendous dietary and healing potential, they are not found in every supermarket you may go to. Just five years ago, they were considered a rarity. And they were very pricey, too. Luckily, today, as people started being more and more aware of their benefits, superfoods have been introduced to many shops and can be easily found online, too. Cheers to that!

So, here we go:

Cacao

The seed of the fruit of an Amazonian tree, cacao is the highest antioxidant food on the planet. It is the number one source of antioxidants, magnesium, iron, manganese, and chromium and is also extremely high in theobromine and anandamide (otherwise known as the "bliss chemical" that produces feelings of happiness). Cacao builds strong bones, elevates your mood and energy, increases longevity, and improves cardiovascular health. It is also a natural aphrodisiac. *Wink, wink.*

Goji Berries

Regarded as a longevity, strength-building, and potency food of the highest order, Goji berries have been used in Traditional Chinese Medicine for over 5,000 years. The Goji Berry, otherwise known as the wolfberry, contains 18 kinds of amino acids, including all 8 essential amino acids, up to 21 trace minerals, high amounts of antioxidants, iron, polysaccharides, B and E vitamins, and many other nutrients. Goji berries can be enjoyed as a healthy snack between meals or used in your choice of smoothies, juices, trail mix, desserts, raw chocolate, and other sweet treats. Goji berries can also be used to prepare a lovely tea.

Maca

Peruvian root vegetable containing a variety of nutrients, such as vitamins, minerals, enzymes, and every essential amino acid. This superfood helps body adapt to stress, it increases energy, endurance, strength, and libido and has been used as a staple food in the Peruvian Andes for thousands of years. Dried maca powder contains more than 10 percent protein, and nearly 20 amino acids, including 7 essential amino acids. The Incas supplied maca to their warriors to increase alertness and provide energy and strength before the battle.

Hemp Seeds

Packed with 33 percent pure digestible protein, hemp seeds are rich in iron, amino acids, and vitamin E, as well as Omega-3. Omega-3 Fatty Acids are important in cell regeneration and healthy brain function. Hemp is also a great food for people who are looking to increase their protein intake.

Spirulina

It's 65 percent protein and amino acids, including the essential fatty acid, gamma-linolenic acid (GLA), which has gotten a lot of attention for its anti-inflammatory properties. Spirulina provides a vast array of minerals, trace elements, phytonutrients, and enzymes. Spirulina is also high in Chlorophyll which helps remove toxins from the blood and boost the immune system.

Honey and Bee Pollen

Honey is a wonderful creation. It has several potential health benefits and plays a role in many home remedies and alternative medicine treatments. In its raw, unfiltered state, honey is rich in minerals, antioxidants, probiotics, and enzymes. It is one of the highest vibration foods (giving life force energy) on the planet. Studies have shown that the propolis in raw honey has antifungal and antibacterial properties.

Bee pollen is a mixture of flower pollen, nectar, enzymes, honey, wax, and bee secretions. It boasts an impressive nutritional profile, containing nearly all B vitamins, especially vitamin B-9 (folate), and all 21 essential amino acids, which makes it a complete protein.

Sea Vegetables (Kelp, Dulse, Nori, Hijiki, Bladderwrack, Chlorella)

Power-packed with nutrients, sea vegetables help remove heavy metals, detoxify the body of radioactive iodine, provide numerous trace minerals, regulate immunity, and decrease the risk of cancer. Seaweeds benefit the entire body and are especially excellent for the thyroid, immune system, adrenals, and hormone function.

Medicinal Mushrooms (Reishi, Chaga, Cordyceps, Maitake, Shiitake, Lion's Mane)

High in polysaccharides and super immune enhancing components, medicinal mushrooms are some of the most intelligent adaptogenic superfoods on the planet! They have also been proven effective in healing cancer and a variety of other ailments.

22

Welcome Aboard This Gym

To Move Is to Live

An inch of movement is better than a mile of intentions.
Unknown

Buckle up, buttercup. Sit back, relax, and continue reading.

AIRCRAFT IS MY GYM AND FLYING IS MY WORKOUT

Skybabe, I have an important question for you. It's your personal perception, so there is no right or wrong here.

Before you close your eyes for a moment and visualize yourself, this is what I would like you to think about and answer to me and you.

When you think of your job and yourself in uniform on board, what is the image that comes to mind?

Now close your eyes and stay like that for five long breaths.

Are you **standing** and **smiling?**

Are you **carrying** a tray full of drinks?

Are you **running** to help a family with a gaggle of kids?

Are you **seated in the galley,** eating, and chatting with your colleagues?

Are you in the cabin with a meal cart, **delivering trays?**

Are you **resting** in your crew rest compartment?

Are you **pushing** and **rearranging bags** to fit into the overhead lockers?

Are you **closing** the overhead lockers before takeoff?

Are you **playing** with kids?

Are you **helping** the elderly reach their seat?

Are you just standing, being beautiful, **doing nothing?**

Are you **carrying** someone's bags?

Are you **selling** Duty Free goodies?

Are you **reassuring** a sick passenger while giving them oxygen?

Are you skillfully moving in the aisle, avoiding all the elbows, heads, and feet sticking out?

Now, when you open your eyes, what do you see? Are you moving or standing still? Are you sitting, standing, walking, running, kneeling? I bet that most of us, *Skybabes,* see themselves as being active, moving swiftly through the cabin.

Out of many jobs in the world, this one is truly physical and requires you to take care of your health and well-being much more than any job on the ground.

Almost every single flight, you chase TIME by its tail. You run to secure the cabin *on time.* You sprint to the toilet, because you *don't have much time.* You rush to finish boarding, so you can *depart on time.* You prepare the galley and service early, so the passengers would eat *in no time.* When someone faints, you get the oxygen bottle, *wasting no time.*

Time seems to be both your best friend and your worst enemy.

Now, what about space? What about other resources?

Very limited, right?

That's why the WAY you move and perform your job becomes even more important than anything else. Or you risk getting an injury in a split of a second.

Skybabe, your job IS a workout. But instead of leggings and trainers, you have your uniform and high-heeled shoes on.

Flight attendant job has all basic human movements.

When delivering casseroles from the meal cart, **you're doing squats and lunges.**

While operating the galley, **you're lifting containers that serve as your weights.**

When boarding passengers and rearranging bags inside the compartments, **you're constantly pushing, pulling, and lifting** them.

Talk about closing doors for departure on Airbus A380? Good luck with that!

But who has ever shown you in detail how to do all this? No one ever! Am I right? Not referring to the door procedures here, of course. We have plenty of that. I'm talking about the actual technique that gets your body to move properly.

No company spends time, attention, and money on this. **They assume you know it.** These are **the basics.** Maybe a few slides, a couple of pages of the manual, one or two demos, but that's it.

So, what is left for you to do?

To take full responsibility and learn everything yourself. Yes, seriously. Because it is your body at the end of the day and you are the one who gets to live with it your whole life.

I know learning these won't be fun, but it's more important than you can imagine! *Scary* important!

Prevention is ALWAYS better than cure.

Actually, prevention *is* the cure.

Prevent injuries from happening by knowing how to move on board while properly taking care of your body. Onboard injuries are no fun and you probably know how long it takes to heal even a tiny sprain. Not to mention that since your livelihood depends on the flight hours you do every month, anytime you're grounded, you lose money. Plus, even after you go back to work, chances are that your body will suffer since it hasn't recovered fully.

The only person who will take care of yourself is YOU. Yes, *you*!

So, **find JOY in movement.** That is the only secret ingredient to consistency and to keeping yourself active for life.

23

This One Calls for Matcha Latte

IT'S TIME TO DO WHAT'S BEST FOR YOU . . . RELAX, REFLECT, RECHARGE

How you treat yourself is how you are inviting the
world to treat you.
Unknown

Hey *amiga,*

When was the last time you took a moment to do something you love? When was the last time you gave yourself permission to rest and relax? How many times have you said, "I wish I had more hours in a day" or "I don't have time for that?"

This was me. *Skybabe* ready to conquer the world. Who rarely listened to her body, pushing herself harder than she knew she could handle.

I remember the morning I woke up jet-lagged and exhausted when I went for a much-needed swim in the sea. A long-overdue swim that I dreamed of for months. Sitting on the beach that early morning, I allowed myself to be fully present and enjoy the beauty and silence around me. Water lapped against the sandy beach, each wave slipping back into the azure with a gentle swoosh. I dove deep into the ocean, feeling the therapeutic effect of water on my whole body, surrendering to the moment. While I kept diving, I couldn't help but think how wonderful it is to be alive, as the sunshine, sea breeze, and early morning stillness helped me restore my energy. I was proud of myself for giving my body what it needed—a revitalizing swim in the sea I didn't have that often. But soon after, I was back in that old vicious cycle with the same excuse I kept telling myself for years.

I'll do it tomorrow. I don't have time for that now.

Still, could it be possible that I didn't have ten minutes just for me? 600 tiny seconds out of 86,400 seconds in a day?

I did have ten minutes. I had thirty minutes and even a few hours to "spare" on myself. The problem was that I never made my well-being a priority, so my days were always hectic and blurry, and my body cried for help. And yet, it was simple. All I needed to do was to get a bit more organized.

So, the first thing I did to make a slight change was to take those ten minutes to myself. I would start by making the time before each flight to go for a run outside or on the treadmill. Those ten minutes would later turn into a full hour of complete empowerment. While I thought before that I deprived myself of sleep by exercising, I later on realized how much more refreshed I felt after working out, which ultimately helped me survive all the long-haul, odd-hour flights.

And I made my mornings special. On my days off, when I didn't have to wake up early, I'd still do it. Not at 4 a.m., of course, but early enough that I'd see the sunrise and walk the empty streets before others woke up. I indulged in taking invigorating morning showers by the open bathroom window above my bathtub while listening to birds chirping on the nearby tree. Then, I'd make myself a nice cup of tea and carry on with my day. The beauty of having a flying schedule is not having to work on weekdays and getting to experience the world around you while everyone else is stuck in their offices, behind their desks.

Skybabe, I want you to know that you don't have to have it all figured out to move forward. Just take the first step and see where it takes you a few days or weeks from today.

These simple daily actions can help you find those ten minutes you need and include them in your busy schedule. And I guarantee you they work. The key is to start today and stay consistent. Because soon, you'll learn that **small daily steps add up to tremendous results.**

1. Rest your legs up on the wall. Just sit on your bed or sofa and lift your legs. This incredible exercise relieves tired leg muscles, calms your body, and quiets your mind.

2. Let out a sigh. Focus on your breathing and release all the tension.

3. Watch the clouds. Wherever you are in the world. Lie on your back and enjoy watching the sky. This was one of my favorite daydreaming activities when I was a child that I still enjoy today.

4. Engage in small acts of kindness. Tape some change to a parking meter or write a thank you note to someone who made your day. Being kind brings us closer to other people and makes us feel incredibly happy and fulfilled. The truth is that once you start doing nice things for others, you won't want to stop. And the kinder you are to others, the more you love and appreciate yourself.

5. Indulge in sound therapy. If you love listening to the sound of the rain on your windowsill, or someone turning the pages of the newspaper, you can easily find these online and listen to them any time of the day. Just set the timer for ten minutes of pure delight and enjoyment.

6. Diffuse some essential oils. Choose any organic essential oil, be it lavender, lemongrass, or eucalyptus, and meditate while enjoying the sweet aroma. Or burn incense.

7. Do some gentle stretching the moment you wake up.

8. Sit on the bench in the park and do some soul searching.

9. Say NO. Remember how easy it is to say no to the things you don't want to do? Just say it, pause, and smile. You'll win every time.

10. Make a spa day at home or simply go to a spa (but make sure you do it, don't just promise yourself you'll do it). Prepare your bath essentials for a magical spa treatment before you leave the house for the day. When you come back in the evening, just light up some candles and enjoy the moment.

11. Write in your journal. Start with describing one of your dreams and why you want to achieve it.

12. Jot down all the negative thoughts on a piece of paper. Write about everything that bothers you. Now burn the paper. It feels great, doesn't it?

13. Find a good podcast that inspires you and listen to it while you exercise or on your way to work.

14. Skip one snack in a day, and appreciate your next meal when you're hungry. Enjoy your meal in silence and focus on chewing your food properly whenever you can.

15. Reconnect with Mother Earth. Put your bare feet on the ground. Take your shoes off and walk barefoot on the grass, sand, gravel or floor.

16. Give yourself a foot massage. Notice how good it feels to give yourself attention.

17. Leave your phone in another room when you go to bed (if you're not on standby and don't have a flight the next day). You'll fall asleep faster and have a much better sleep during the night.

18. Declutter one drawer in your home. You'll feel great when you organize things you've been putting on hold for so long. After you finish one, you'll want to do more. And remember, clutter is nothing more than postponed decisions.

19. Schedule your playtime. Whatever you enjoy doing, be it playing with a pet, jumping on a trampoline, rollerblading, singing or karaoke, make sure you add it to your schedule.

20. Add one slight change to an already established habit. Before you brush your teeth, make sure you floss. When you wake up and stretch, remember to drink a glass of water. Stacking habits together creates amazing results.

21. Revisit your goals and dreams. What's been on your mind forever, but you actually never wanted to pursue? Cross it off the list and focus on what you genuinely want to do.

22. Cook a healthy meal the day before. Enjoy a yummy lunch the next day without having to worry about what to eat.

23. Write ten things you are grateful for. Think of everything that you have now and how much you wished for it before you had it. Be thankful for every single step you took and for every accomplishment in your life so far.

24. Prepare your uniform or outfit for the next day the night before and enjoy a few more minutes of sleep.

25. Remember to drink enough water throughout the day. Add a few fresh mint leaves to your water to make it even tastier.

26. Identify significant time wasters and stop doing them. How often do you check your email? Do you tend to stare at your phone just to check for updates? Use that extra time to do any of the things you love above.

27. When you get out of bed, **say THANK YOU three times and smile!**

28. When you step out of the house, **greet the new day with a big smile!**

29. When you feel heavy and can't seem to find a way to get rid of all the negative energy and thoughts, **go on a swing and fly.** Trampolines help, too!

30. Open your windows, let fresh air into your room. Accept the positive energy coming your way.

31. When all you need is a hug, **hug yourself.** But if that isn't enough, go to the nearest toy store, find the biggest teddy bear, and hug it for as long as you need to.

32. Buy yourself a bouquet of fresh flowers.

33. Don't wait for a special day. Every day is special. Wear those brand-new shoes right now. Enjoy listening to the sound of your footsteps in those sexy heels.

Listen to what your body tells you, *Skybabe*. Know your limits and embrace them so that you never cross that line where you push yourself too hard and live on the last atoms of strength that you keep reusing.

Remember that it's never too early or too late to start working on being the healthiest you. And if you're still wondering why you should make time for yourself, think of it this way:

Because *you* are important. Because no matter how busy life gets, you come first, *Skybabe*. No one is ever going to take care of you as well as you do.

Now, choose three things from the list and do them today.

SELF-LOVE

Self-care is giving the world the best of you, instead of what's left of you.
Katie Reed

24

Hold Your Well-Being Sacred

TAKE CARE OF YOURSELF FIRST

> Self-care is not about self-indulgence. It's about
> self-preservation.
> *Audrey Lorde*

Hey pumpkin,

Still having fun? I bet you are.

Look, I know what you're thinking. Being a flight attendant must be glorious. Your only job is to smile, always look perfectly groomed, and make sure no passenger gets thrown out of the aircraft, no matter how much they may get on your nerves.

Well, where do I start?

I think both you and I know there's a lot more to good looks than simply putting on your makeup and fixing up your hair. You are a woman worthy of her dreams, your big life, and you matter. So, what you have inside means so much more than your good looks and the type of body you have.

Right. Tell that to flight attendant recruiters who roam the world looking for one-size-fits-all *Skybabes* and *Skydudes*. Beauty, looks, smarts, wits, and not to mention a thirst for adventure. I can tell you firsthand, because I worked as one. I traveled wide and far to find candidates who would physically and mentally fit the image of an "ideal" flight attendant. This was not always easy because there were strict rules we had to abide by. And sometimes, no matter how much I liked a candidate, how much I thought they'd be perfect for the job, if they didn't tick all the boxes on the checklist, it was as simple as, *"Adios muchachos!"*

Anyhoo, going back to the topic of our conversation. Beauty. I won't and do not wish to go deeper into the topic as I know there are as many opinions as there are humans on this planet, so if I started, we'd probably never finish this book.

The kind of beauty I want to talk about here is the one we see. What is visible to the eye before anyone gets a chance to speak to you and get to know you better. I know it sounds shallow, but it's real. And I swear, sometimes when I worked long days screening candidates in the most interesting places in the world, I felt like Steve Harvey during one of those Miss Universe contests. All I could do was smile and enjoy the process.

And we need to talk about this because this is what people see when they first set eyes on you as they board the plane.

So, before I begin, I want to make one thing clear. **You were born to be real,** *Skybabe.* **Not perfect.** And the moment you decide to be the amazing, wonderful *you* who loves and trusts herself, your beauty starts to show.

BUT FIRST, SKINCARE

The cosmetics industry bombards us with a barrage of new makeup, nutrition, fitness, and hair products that come out daily. But knowing your beauty priorities and where your time, money and efforts go is equally important. Now, I'm not going to try to make you change your mind about your favorite makeup or shampoo brand, but I'll put in my two cents and share with you how this influenced my health while flying.

Let's start with the biggest organ in your body. *Chicas,* not that one. I'm talking about your skin. Yes, your precious skin that absorbs anything from body butters and moisturizing lotions to harmful gases and pollutants in the air we breathe.

Naturally, the quality of your skin will depend on your age, level of fitness, your daily diet, and where you live in the world. Of course, what you do for a living matters and that's why we're here.

Since we have less time nowadays to do what we want but get more stressed with each new day, this can all influence how we behave and live our lives day to day. Whether you follow beauty trends or try out every single product that comes on the market, you still have a say in all this because **your body** means **your rules.** Since I started my flying career, I've straightened, twisted and colored my hair, my skin was slathered with mud masks, nutritional clay, tea tree oil, caffeine scrubs, slimy deep green seaweed facial treatments, and the most expensive makeup I could find. Think Duty Free shopping in between flights. Beauty products galore! A lot to spend your hard-earned money on. And I mean, A LOT.

I remember buying every single beauty magazine at the airport while waiting for my flight. I loved to read about the latest trends, and research and learn new ways to stay healthy and young. But most of the time, what I got was just another way to persuade me to buy more.

So, naturally, I'd buy those products, starting with several at the same time, only to give up after a few weeks. I can't tell you how many times I bought a face cream without testing it first. Once, I even developed a nasty rash that cost me my flight. It was *that* serious.

So, be mindful about what you put on your body.

I battled with **unclear and blemished skin** for quite some time even though my whole life up until my flying career, I had a perfectly smooth and spotless complexion. Flying takes a toll on your skin whether you like to admit it or not. And my aim has always been to find the root cause, not just fix what is visible on the outside. Still, imagine going inside a full cabin with a giant zit on your forehead with no makeup on your tired face at three o'clock in the morning. *Eek!*

The problem I had at the time was that even though I had a makeup removal routine after returning from a flight, whether to a hotel room or my home, I didn't take it too seriously. I thought just removing makeup was enough, then I'd go outside with no sunscreen on to the point of having scorching red blotches on my forehead and nose that later on left permanent scars on my face.

And it wasn't just beauty products. It was so much more than that. The food I ate, how often I exercised, and what I allowed to go into my body without thinking. Talk about a one-pound chocolate bar eaten in one go, after a fourteen-hour flight from Australia. Followed by a tub of choc chip ice cream and an oolong tea. I know it sounds crazy, but it was my reality for quite some time.

So, you can't just do one good thing today and forget about your skin and body tomorrow. It doesn't work that way. And we're all guilty of it. We start with a diet. We watch what we eat. We hydrate ourselves regularly. But the first time we get shaken up by something not in our usual routine, we give up. What's the point when we already screwed up, right?

But boo, you know that nothing happens overnight. The key here is to stay disciplined, persistent, and patient.

Of course, that's not all. One thing I suffered with the most were **dry hands.** As a germophobe who liked everything spick and span on board, I'd wash my hands hundreds of times during the flight. And this was before alcohol-based hand sanitizers became a thing. Plus, I'm not a big fan of those because the alcohol in them dries out your hands even more. Still, imagine having such rough skin on your fingertips that if you glided your palm along your leg, your stockings would rip. And I'm not talking about shiny silk pantyhose, but the ones I specifically wore when flying—the compression stockings that you could easily wash in the washing machine over and over again. The thick, granny kind.

Slathering my hands in glycerin creams and then covering them with white cotton gloves overnight worked like magic during the time I wasn't flying, but the moment I'd return to work, the same thing would happen again.

And you know what else, *Skybabe*? **Headaches.** I even experienced harsh migraines when flying on smaller aircraft above 40,000 feet. But that's a whole 'nother story. Cooling masks or dipping eye pads in cold chamomile tea helps while resting. Gel masks work well, too. You can bring them with you wherever you go.

Now let me give you some examples of the things you can incorporate in your life that will help you stay beautiful and healthy inside and out:

Schedule doctor's appointments. Even if you feel amazing and don't think you need to see your physician, get a yearly blood test to make sure everything is fine. Visit your gynecologist to know the condition of your reproductive organs. Your *vagoo* will thank you later. Be aware of any risks that come with the job in order for you to prevent a disease or a health issue. Being physically and mentally healthy will keep you on top of your game in all other aspects of life.

Visit your dentist. For regular checkups and teeth cleaning, it won't take you longer than half an hour per visit. Imagine 30 minutes out of 525,600 you get in a year. Nothing, right? So, go get yourself an appointment. Electric and sonic toothbrushes may be a great option if you don't enjoy brushing your teeth. They are better than the manual ones and can reach farther between your teeth to remove plaque. Oh, and flossing is a must.

Create a skincare routine. If your current routine consists of washing your face before putting galore of makeup on or removing makeup in the evening, your skin is screaming for more! It's not just about the products and how you can spend more money on chemicals your body and skin don't need. It's about simple massages, the right eye cream, and toxin-free makeup you use every day.

Here's what I mean: **Lead.**

Yes, that **harmful chemical element your body cannot metabolize.** Unlike most other toxins that your body can eliminate through excretion, your body has no ability to purge lead.

I'm serious. Lead can be found in many products, from children's toys, furniture, plumbing products to cosmetics and even water. *Yikes!*

Our detailed research led us to the FDA website to find out if and how much lead is allowed in cosmetic products. Numbers don't lie. Some of the top-selling makeup brands have the highest levels of lead in them. So, do your research, *Skybabe*. Some studies show that, on average, a woman eats approximately three pounds of lipstick in her lifetime. THREE POUNDS? Imagine that! That's more than three giant *Toblerone* bars of lipstick! *Yuck!*

So now that you know that a certain amount of lead is allowed in your makeup, wouldn't you think twice before putting that newest velvety lipstick on your lips? I think so, too.

This is not just about the superficial attractiveness of your face and body, but the deeper, more fulfilling beauty of mind and spirit. Of who you are. How you think and move, what you feed your brain and body with, what you do for your soul, how you protect your energy, and, of course, the health and beauty of your skin and face.

Now, here's some more food for thought:

- **How well do you know your skin?**

- **Do you buy popular products because of the hype?**

- **Do you do your research and check the ingredients beforehand? If so, what do you look for on the ingredient list?**

- **How much skincare is too much?**

25

Becoming Werewolf

SMOOTH, GENTLE, HAIRLESS SKIN

I love how prickly your legs feel — said no one ever.

Hey boo,

How's it going? Now I got somethin' in store for ya.

So, in this specific period, my airline established some pretty strict rules on image and grooming standards for women (I cringe just saying those words), and how we should all look in our uniforms while on duty. The bullet-point rules, all nicely presented in a small booklet we had to carry in our cabin bags at all times, resembled Milano fashion show guidelines more than the ones of *Skybabes*.

Hello airport catwalk! Here we come! Level up, glitz up, and glam up all the way!

Having the role of a grooming inspection officer under my professional hat, I had to pay special attention to all the details in the manual, making sure my crew met the standards on every flight. As a woman, I didn't need a manual for female hygiene and looks. It was common sense.

But as it turned out, I was dead wrong.

Are you hanging in there, buttercup? Okay, here we go.

On our way to Bangladesh, as the head of a bunch of different individuals whom I would usually meet for the first time just before the flight during the safety briefing, I always tried to get to know my people. I could scan them in and out, briefly and efficiently, in a heartbeat, so I could have a clear picture of the strengths and weaknesses within the team. That included everything from their image and body language to safety, security, communication style, and medical knowledge—you name it.

But the first thing I would notice was ... their overall physical appearance.

I know this may sound strange, but this was the nature of the job and since we were the last point of contact with customers before they ended their journey, we had to follow these strict airline-set grooming rules.

On that day, one hardworking newbie particularly caught my eye. She was a fresh daisy in the company and had been flying for just over six months. Cute and welcoming, with a huge smile on her face, she was quite difficult to miss. And not only because of her sweet smile, but also because I couldn't help but notice that her skin was covered with hair. Not just her arms, but her upper lip, chin, eyebrows, and legs, too. And when I say hair—I mean thick, perky, cactus-torn-like hair. And it was e-v-e-r-y-w-h-e-r-e.

Deeply embarrassed for both of us, I soon realized that I was the one who'd have to address the issue. How the hell do you tell another woman she's becoming a werewolf without being direct yet indiscrete and polite? How do you state the obvious without demotivating her and diminishing her work performance? The last thing I wanted was to make her feel sad and uncomfortable.

Questions rumbled inside my head, but soon enough, I made peace with the decision I'd made earlier to just ignore it. She'd find out eventually and I was sure there was someone who'd break the news to her in a much smoother and easier manner. Yeah, that was it. *Phew!*

Relaxed and happy with my decision, I continued on to the cockpit. But the moment I came back to the aft galley, the inevitable happened. I had this uncontrollable urge to talk to her. As a woman to a woman, or a friend to a friend, not as a senior to a junior colleague at work. I just couldn't let it go.

As if pushed by some invisible force toward her, I stepped in front of the girl so suddenly that I even scared myself. *Ta-na-na-na!*

I threw one question out, like rolling dice in a game of cards, allowing her to take over and make the rest of the moves. I wanted to hear her talk since I was in no mood for giving my juicy multi-layered hairy feedback.

To my politeness, professionalism, and reassuring gestures, she simply chuckled with her hand over her mouth. At first, I thought this sweet girl had it all mixed up and did not get my point, but as I continued to listen, a whole new world opened up in front of me.

"In the village where I come from, body hair is considered a nice feminine feature to have. The only time I had to remove my hair was when I joined the company. I guess it's time to do it again, since you're the first one to draw my attention to it."

I sat in front of her, shaking my head in disbelief. Not because of the tradition she just told me about, but because she hadn't even thought of doing it again. *Skybabe,* do you know how much time it takes for hair to grow? No frigging time! You shave the night before the flight, and the next morning, they're peeking their buds out. So, you can just imagine, after half a year, what a hairy werewolf she was growing into.

And just when I was at the edge of being a little too indiscrete to add how even her potential future partner surely wouldn't like it, she surprised me again. What she said next hit me like a bucket of ice-cold water. Her cheeks, now burnished red apples, smiled at me together with her bright white teeth. With a shy smile, she murmured, "My boyfriend adores my hair everywhere on me."

Talk about cultural differences and descriptive examples? Well, this one nailed it.

What was I supposed to say? What would *you* say?

I was speechless. But I was relieved as well. And I know there are some of you who say that nurturing a natural look is important, and that body hair has its purpose. Yes, I agree, although partially. And with all due respect, I will humbly stick to my opinion and suggest the following:

Shave.

Remove hair with an electric hair removal machine. If you're worried about the pain, rest assured that the pain is bearable and many girls say they easily get used to it. The results are excellent and there is a high-quality choice on the market now. This option is a one-time financial investment and you have to do it yourself every time. You should know that the pain, while using it, increases as you approach your period. It's very useful to have on vacations, as it doesn't take up a lot of space and solves most of your "hair problems" easily.

Use waxing strips. You can get them in a pharmacy or any well-equipped supermarket. Visit salons and have waxing done for you. A popular option some years ago, but still exists in many salons. Choose your salon lady wisely, as this can hugely affect the pain level and the effectiveness of the method.

Do laser hair removal. This is a long-term, most sustainable solution. Make sure you do the research for your skin type, machines that the clinic uses, the age and the usage of the lamps, what to do/not to do after and before the treatment—especially related to sun exposure. Many *Skybabes* successfully do their laser hair removal while on layovers. If it is too expensive in the country you live in, do a brief research and try to organize your laser treatment in a destination from your current roster list (another one of those glorious job perks). The good thing about laser is that it doesn't have to be done frequently, so it is very easy to plan. You may need as little as six to seven sessions. It can be a hefty investment, but it's worth it. For *Skybabes* with darker skin and hair tones, this option might be more limited, as the laser works best on lighter skin combined with dark hair. Nevertheless, do your research and give it a try.

26

Oops! Is That Red Thong Mine?

The Unnecessarily Messy Chapter

Never underestimate the power of good lingerie on
a bad day.
Unknown

Chérie,

Imagine this.

You're ten years old, first to enter the class. Sneaking a look through the heavy classroom door, you notice your elementary school teacher sitting at a large wooden desk. Crazier than a sackful of raccoons, she's thoroughly immersed in marking those essays, whizzing that red pen across the paper, grumbling under her breath. The classroom is so quiet you can hear a pin drop.

Your empty stomach rumbles like the darkening sky outside and before you can take a step back, the door makes a cracking sound, and she shoots up an eyebrow. Peering through her foggy specs, she gives you a scornful look. "Get inside and show me your homework."

Then another student shows up and the story repeats.

This is what some of my early school days looked like, more than a few decades ago.

Now picture this.

I'm standing in the middle of the briefing room, checking if flight attendants have all the necessary items and documents in their cabin bags before each flight. I am only missing a nice pair of specs to be entirely like my school teacher. I'm not as grumpy, of course, but I have the infamous red pen on me. It's always there. Hard to fight those quirky, nerdy habits, even when flying.

One by one, my colleagues enter the briefing room. They approach me for a human eye scan and show me all the uniform items they have on themselves or inside their carry-on trolleys. I inspect their documents, makeup, shoes, as well as their overall appearance. Looking at their perfectly polished nails, trimmed beards, the right highlights in their hair, matching shade of socks, bra color, and (un)ironed uniform.

And while I'm good at my job, I feel terrible just thinking about this—why can't everyone be responsible for what they look like and spare me the embarrassment? They are adults, not kids. They know how to take care of themselves. This is basic hygiene. For sure they do, I suppose as I roll my eyes behind those imaginary glasses with a sense of discomfort.

After I check the last crew who entered the room, we all sit down like perfect students and wait for the Purser to start the briefing. It seems familiar, as if we're traveling in time. Different characters, similar circumstances.

I set my hands on the table and lean back in my chair with a big sigh of relief.

But wait. Something tells me we're not all there and I recount. One crew's missing. I count again. *Merde!* Cold sweat trickles down my back, but I manage to keep it cool.

The Purser closes the door only to be hit by it with a force of a hurricane. Like a thunder, a girl rumbles into the room, followed by a cloud of stale cigarette odor—a detail hard to miss, besides her smeared red lipstick and a high sticking French roll. With the skills of a circus juggler, she swings her trolley bag in the air with one hand, catches it with the other, and zip opens the pocket, shoving her hand inside. She's searching for her shoes as if digging for her house keys from the bottom of a giant grocery bag. Frowning, she pushes, shakes, and yanks the items inside, then finally takes one shoe out and shows it to me.

Yep, I knew it. Anything but clean. Stinky, squashed, shapeless, covered with stains of tomato juice and dashes of milk. Colorful and perfectly disgusting! No canvas or plastic shoe bag. Her shoes mingled with her manuals, makeup bag, and other belongings. Then, as I patiently wait, she takes out the second shoe with an alluring ornament hanging on the side – tangled red thong undies. And I'm talking tiny, lacy, G-string panties. Yes, for real!

She didn't look too concerned even though the entire room started giggling, but quickly shoved the panties back in her bag and continued to her seat. Speechless for a few awkward moments, I turned to her and smiled. "Getting a shoe bag would help. And bravo on the color. Red is always a good choice!"

What else could I have said?

Truth be told, I don't know if it was for my mom and her meticulous rules for every teeny tiny detail in this world, but I am pretty sure she could take the blame for creating and developing my personal shoe-packing philosophy, among others. Whenever I would pack my clothes and shoes together for occasional trips, our weekend countryside getaways or my dancing rehearsals – it was an absolute MUST to have a separate bag for my shoes. Even for my towel and clothes. And my panties and socks. There was no way I could dump everything together without getting a reproaching look, discouraging me from repeating the same mistake again. So, I didn't. With the exception that now I minimize the use of plastic, compared to before.

Skybabe, don't let this be you. Do you know how disgustingly dirty your shoes are?

Go ahead, take a wild guess. Shoes carry and transfer dirt, bacteria, and everything else that tags along. Literally. Think about that invisible wave of paper stuck on your heel after you've left the toilet. Mud, concrete, gravel, public toilets, bars, offices, buses, aircraft aisles, galleys, etc. Germs galore!

Clean your shoes and keep them separate from the rest of your clothes. While this story relates to shoes and packing, it doesn't stop there. The same way you probably keep your cosmetics in a separate pouch, you might as well organize your extra pantyhose, underwear, pajamas, and medications in a few small bags. Handy, clean, and tidy. Your cabin bag should have the minimum, but make sure you have all the necessities you might need in case of delays, diversions, and emergencies.

And the next time you lift your suitcase and put it on your bed to pack, think twice. Wherever your shoes go, your suitcase follows. Those wheels have seen places and they're anything but clean.

Skybabes are ready for anything that comes their way. Keep it simple and practical. And if red thong panties are your necessity, then be it. I support it 100 percent! Just make sure you keep your undies clean and pack them separately.

27

Swisssss Cheese Stockings

THE FAMOUS LADDER PANTYHOSE

I don't like wearing pantyhose ... every time I fart, I
blow my slippers off!
Aunty Acid

Chica,

What is the one thing that never goes well with the flight attendant uniform?

Swollen feet and ankles!

Whether you're on a quick turnaround or a long-haul flight across the ocean, extended stretches of time on your feet and changes in air pressure can cause uncomfortable—and sometimes dangerous—swelling.

Feet swell when you fly because blood has to fight against gravity to travel up through your legs. Technically, this is referred to as gravitational edema. Whether sitting for long periods of time like pilots and passengers or standing for hours like flight attendants, blood begins to pool at the point furthest from your heart and closest to the earth.

Your feet.

I don't believe there is a single *Skybabe* soul who hasn't had these challenges in her flying career. And, oh, boy! They can be challenging, indeed.

I remember, when flying, the thought of how much fortune I spent on pantyhose drove me bananas. For years, I'd use a pair for just a few times, only to see it tear during the flight. Imagine the frustration! I would accidentally brush my leg off the seat Velcro strap. Or my broken nail (hello, it happened every day!) would start an unwanted string along my thigh. Or I would pull them up forcefully after going to the toilet in a rush and easily make a ladder-like tear.

It took me quite some time to understand that I actually had an issue with my big toe on my left foot and the shape of its *pobresito* nail. So all the pantyhose I'd ever worn never survived more than two flights. That naughty guy would destroy every single pair, and the way I stepped on my toes while walking didn't help. That's when I thought the thick supportive stockings were the only solution for me. But when I tried them, I simply couldn't stand the feeling of being so constricted.

Oh, the problems of *Skybabes!* These really are unique to us. We're probably one of the rare species who can understand one another, knowing exactly what we go through on every flight. Not to mock our fellow *Skydudes* in any way, but we just want to show how challenging it is to be a woman on board sometimes. Have you ever tried to take off your sports bra after a good sweaty workout or fly on the first day of your period? Yeah, the fun never stops! And this usually happens behind the scenes while *Skybabes* smile and pretend that life's all roses and unicorns.

Don't forget to give yourself a pat on the back, *Skybabe!*

So, the question here is: compression stockings or regular panty-hose? There are as many opinions as there are brands available. After doing research among *Skybabes*, plus exploring different brands, materials, and textures, we learned that compression stockings can:

- improve circulation

- prevent varicose and spider veins

- reduce swelling

- decrease your chances of blood clots and DVT (Deep Vein Thrombosis)

- improve muscle energy

So, whichever type of stockings you decide to wear or are already wearing, do not allow your legs to look like Swiss cheese with holes all around them. We've seen that and we've seen it a lot. And the only place they belong is in a Tom & Jerry cartoon, not on board an aircraft where you want to shine and feel your best while working.

Nice and high-quality pantyhose are a good investment in you. They'll help you feel better and sexier. Trust me, you're doing yourself and your stunning legs a huge favor.

Now that we've covered pantyhose, let's talk about the best way to wear them. While protecting your legs and your overall body is important, don't forget about one of the most important parts. Your *vajayjay*.

And I know it can be so tempting to wear that sexy, new lingerie you bought recently on your layover, but anything but cotton will put your vaginal pH balance out of whack.

How to protect yourself? For example, wear granny panties.

I'm serious. Granny knows best!

So, they look ugly. Who cares? No one can see them but you. And they're not just comfy, but they also protect your natural flora during flying.

Look, I know it all seems good until something goes wrong. Even if you regularly take care of your intimate hygiene, there are things that can offset potentially annoying and dangerous diseases. If you're seriously itchy down there and you have no idea why, there might be something completely simple that can be treated. What's causing the itchy feeling could be your nylon tights. This might be horrible to hear, but they are the reason for frequent yeast infections that may often leave you feeling uncomfortable. The synthetic material of your stockings keeps warmth and moisture, which allows bacteria and yeast to thrive. But for most healthy women, wearing them with cotton underwear won't cause a problem.

28

The Boob Saga

Give Your Girls the Support They Need

Of course I have flaws. But my boobs usually distract
people from them.
Unknown

So, munchkin,

Let's talk about airbags.

No, not those. I mean your chi chis. Bikini stuffers. *Muchachas*.
Knockers.

Okay, boobies. Let's talk about your boobs.

You know, when you fly, they fly, too. Talk about the law of gravity.

Now, when it comes to flying, things get a bit more complicated.
Because, cabin pressure. Tight fitting uniform. Eyes gawking everywhere.

When flying, you can't wear just any kind of bra. Some are
unforgiving. If you wear the lace, nice looking ones that push your
melones up high, you're gonna get the looks. Your traffic stoppers
will attract the attention of even the unruliest passengers. While

this is cool, and it certainly works, it won't change the fact that you need to support your girls well when you fly.

I'd love to tell you it would be cool to wear that satin lace bra you'd wear on a first date with a smoking hot dude, but nope, that's not the case.

Sports bras that look just like regular high support bras may be the way to go. They keep things intact. But you know the thing with sports bras, they're not always best-looking, but they do offer excellent support. In case you need to run, give someone CPR or stroll down the aisle, a sports bra is your best friend. Plus, you won't have any unwanted stares from perverted onlookers.

Anyway, I remember one time I was called from a standby to cover a flight to Mauritius. While I wasn't particularly fond of waking up in the dead of night to operate a flight, I was looking forward to the time I would spend there.

The resort we stayed in was the epitome of luxury. With uninterrupted views of the Indian Ocean, in an insanely beautiful spot with a huge infinity pool, exquisitely landscaped grounds, and gorgeous bungalow-like rooms, the place exuded serenity and calmness. So, upon arriving, I decided to try the newly opened spa, and get one of those famous sunset massages by the ocean. The only problem was that on the day I arrived, the space was reserved for couples' massages only.

I stared at the spa receptionist, then glanced at the gorgeous beach and the cabana with two beautifully inviting massage beds. She had an opening that evening and I wasn't going to lose my chance, so I booked it. Now all I needed to find was a boyfriend who'd go with me. Traveling with an army of like-minded people, it wasn't that difficult for me to find a *Skydude* who would share a bed with me. Massage bed, that is.

Anyhoo, a colleague of mine who worked in the same cabin, accepted my invitation and soon we found ourselves in the changing room for couples. *Scheiße!* I did not expect this.

As I went in, I realized that I'd have to change in front of a man I did not know that well. It was awkward. And uncomfortable. But thankfully, this was a five-star resort with plenty of space inside the spa that I didn't have to worry about ever seeing my imaginary partner until we got to our massage beds. And being the gentleman that he was, my colleague gave me some space to change. So, while he was in the bathroom, I took off my clothes, wrapped myself in a towel, and scooted down to the fluffy massage bed. Soon after, the massage started, and we were both grateful we took a shot at this—the golden sunset and those skillful masseuse's hands.

As I sank deep into my relaxation, I completely forgot about the time, until the masseuse gently tapped me on my shoulder and told me that my husband had already left. It took a moment for me to realize where I was and that jet lag had eaten my sanity. With a smile, I grabbed the towel and hopped off the bed.

Feeling woozy and energized, both at the same time, I went inside to change. There I was, rekindling the joy of life and rejuvenating my soul, completely unaware that my *brassiere* was hanging in our joint changing room. Which meant that my colleague saw it, too. Double *scheiße!*

Yes, the bra was comfortable and supportive, and just plain ugly. Talk about embarrassment.

On my way out, I saw my colleague sitting casually in the spa lounge, sipping his jasmine tea. He invited me to join him, but remembering that he saw my scruffy old bra hanging on the changing room door sure made me want to melt into the floor and slither away. Still, knowing that he helped me and that we both got what we wanted, I sat down beside him for a cup of delicious tea.

From that moment on, I stopped the rubbish and invested in several good-quality bras. Yes, the ones that keep things tight while looking nice. Always be prepared, *Skybabe,* because you never know who might be there to save you if you ever fainted. Perhaps a sexy, gorgeous hunk? *Wink!*

So the next time you worry about your *muchachas*, just go get yourself something nice to wear. I promise you that you won't regret it. Having a good quality support bra is extremely important, especially when flying. Even when I travel as a passenger, I still make sure I wear a comfortable bra with excellent support.

Get fitted by a pro. The bra professional will help you find the perfect fit and will even give you tips on how to up or downsize depending on the shape of your breasts. I'm certain most women know their bra size. Someone once told them or they thought something fit right. But often, one bra size doesn't always work for all types of bras. Trial and error. It took me years to take this step and make it work. And when I finally did, my *lolas* were happy.

Splurge a little. Buy good quality bras you'll only wear when flying. Trust me, it pays off. They will last you longer and you will be happy with the support they give you. It's worth spending a bit more on a perfectly fitting, high-quality bra that will provide the lift you want and the comfort you definitely need up in the sky.

If you can, stay away from tight fitting under-wire bras. Pushups are fine on a date, but not up in the sky.

WHAT TO WEAR WHEN FLYING AS A PASSENGER

For long-haul flights and when you know you'll be stuck inside the giant tube for over four hours, wear layered clothing. The air temperature on airplanes is controlled, but sometimes it gets too hot or more often, too cold. Not all airlines will provide you with a blanket, so make sure you come prepared (unless you're traveling Business or First).

Bring a scarf with you. It's not just trendy, but it can also help you stay warm throughout the flight. It can also serve as a pillow or a blanket when you want to snooze, or a cloak of invisibility if you're by any chance seated next to a chatty passenger you don't want to talk to.

Yoga and jogger pants are your best friends when flying. Anything without a zipper, and that isn't too constricting around your tummy. Make sure they are loose fitting and don't have any ropes or elastic cuffs to stop your circulation mid-flight.

It sure is nice to throw on a nifty bodycon dress and a pair of stilettos when you're going out on a date. But maybe stay away from these when flying. Tight fitting and high-heeled shoes are not the way to go. Think lightweight shoes and sneakers. Your feet expand during the flight and by the time you reach your destination, you won't be the same person. Your hoofs won't fit into those cute shoes anymore. Remember Cinderella's stepsister, Drizella?

And finally, don't forget a clean pair of fluffy socks. They're comfortable and cute and absolutely necessary. Take your shoes off, put your socks on, dab some moisturizer and settle down for a movie or a good read. When you fly, it's important to stay comfortable while still looking fashionable (if you know what I mean).

29

Stuck in Paradise

BRAVING THE WILDERNESS IN MY FIVE-STAR JUNGLE HUT

Paradise isn't a place. It's a feeling.
Unknown

"Breathe in. Breathe out. And again, deep breath in and a deep breath out."

The soft, comforting voice of our yoga instructor filled my mind with ease. The warm breeze caressed my skin as the whisper of the lush tree leaves and spring water nearby tickled my ears. The rays of sun peeked through the white net above the *shala*, creating shadows on the thick wooden floor, making this special moment even more magical.

Our yoga retreat center, the very special place on this glorious planet, was a green sanctuary in the middle of a lush Balinese jungle.

I needed time away. I so desperately wanted to disappear from all the distractions in my life and experience the simple life in an open-air bungalow at the core of Mother Nature. On my way there, I imagined myself indulging in nurturing, organic food, sipping pure spring water, strolling through an abundant forest, and swimming in cascading waterfalls.

A true paradise for mind, body, and soul.

There were around twenty people in our group, including a good friend of mine. While the retreat was only five days long, it brought numerous benefits and positive changes. My body started strengthening already after the second day. I felt better and more relaxed compared to the first day. My muscles began opening and my breathing became deeper. I felt so calm, peaceful, and joyful to be there with her and share that experience together. I actually only really wanted to talk to her as I wasn't interested in socializing with others.

After the yoga class, I sat on my mat, dappled by sunlight, overlooking the gorgeous jungle. Slowly getting lost in my thoughts, I enjoyed the pristine silence after everyone left. I jotted a few thoughts in my journal, amazed at how much clarity and peace came to me after only a few classes of yoga and meditation.

Just what I needed.

While everyone eagerly waited for the mealtime to sit together and get to know one another, I looked for spaces where I could have some privacy without having to engage in a conversation. There was nothing wrong there, but looking at it now, this was absolutely not typical for me.

I'm a chatterbox who loves meeting and learning about new people, exchanging ideas, thoughts, and opinions on various topics. But during this retreat, I was singing a different tune. I saw this as a mini vacation in between my packed flying duties and time off I could never get enough. The only thing I needed was to REST. My body and my mind. To regain energy and recharge batteries, so I could again become that famous Duracell bunny who never, ever gets tired and stops. That's all I asked for. But meeting new people on my retreat only meant putting more effort and giving energy that I didn't have.

To my surprise, on the last day, after dinner, the instructor gathered us all to hear our impressions about the retreat and anything we would like to share. While listening to others speak about the new acquaintances they'd made and how happy they were, I started realizing how they all craved human connection.

But not me.

They all wanted to be together and talk.

I avoided it.

They loved the enormous group and constant chatting.

I ran away from it.

I'm sure I looked a bit like a freak to them, but when it was my turn to speak, the words just rolled out of my mouth.

"Dear yogis, I thoroughly enjoyed the retreat and the atmosphere we all created during our yoga classes. I am so sorry I didn't socialize much with anyone except with my friend and that I looked like I was avoiding you the whole time. Because—I probably did. This has nothing to do with you, but all I needed was peace and calm without too many people around."

I went on explaining how my job required spending most of my work time being surrounded by hundreds of people. A few of the yogis gave me that knowing look, as if saying they'd finally realized why I didn't want to sit with them. They understood me well and, more importantly, I understood myself. It was like finding a secret passcode to the safe I wanted to take something from. I now had it in my hands. I discovered it. And whenever I felt depleted, all I had to do was enter the right passcode, get into the safe, and take some more of my life force. I was happy to have been able to decipher the secret to my energy refill that I started believing that yoga, meditation, and breathing are practices I'd keep doing for life.

While this is just one of my personal ways how I recuperate, I strongly believe everyone has their own, deep inside of them. The places where only peace and calm live and where they can soak up and refill the energy they need.

Skybabe, here are a few questions:

- **When do you crave peace and quiet the most?**

- **How do you recharge your energy?**

And remember, *Skybabe,* if you don't like what you see, rewrite it. The power is in YOU.

30

Never Underestimate the Power of Jet Lag

HEY, SLEEPY HEAD, ARE YOU SNOOZING?

> Don't worry about the world ending today, it's already tomorrow in Australia.
> *Charles M. Schulz*

We've just arrived in the hotel lobby in Brisbane, Australia. Everyone is taking their room keys, exhausted from the ultra-long intercontinental flight we all did together.

I'm ecstatic to be there, with a what-to-do and where-to-go lists already diligently prepared and taken from Wikipedia the night before. For the record, at the time, Trip Advisor didn't exist, and no Google Maps or similar apps were available. We didn't have Wi-Fi at every corner. And *no*, I'm not 100 years old!

Technology is sprinting forward.

As I had just started flying, everything seemed thrilling, new, and calling my name to explore and discover.

While taking our suitcases and making our way to the rooms, I announced to my colleagues what I was planning to do and asked if they wanted to join. Since I'd always had a gift for itinerary planning, nothing was too complicated for me to arrange. I quickly threw myself into gathering phone numbers and other details so we could all go together and enjoy sightseeing.

At that very moment, through my own rumbling with other crew members, I overheard my senior say to the flight deck crew, "I'm just gonna crash in bed."

Not that I was eavesdropping, but what I just heard made me roll my eyes openly while my jet-lagged brain battled with my never-ending inner monologue. *Did I hear that right?*

She came to sunny Australia! The weather couldn't be more perfect. Bustling streets swarming with people, shops wide open, and yummy food everywhere! Air pure and clean, breathtaking and eye-soothing vegetation. And the ocean? Ah, the ocean! So bright and blue!

Is she really going to stay in her room and do nothing? Can this be possible?

I stood there in disbelief for a few long moments and then rushed off to my room. I remember one thought clearly passing through my head: when you get to that stage where you don't want to move your bum to get a breath of fresh air and all you care about is sleep, that will be the time for you to leave your flying career.

And I must admit. I did judge that senior. Hard. I thought it was impossible to feel the way she did. I couldn't understand why and how she could ever say that. I thought she was just lazy and uninspired. But year after year, and then after ten long years of flying, I understood her. More than I care to admit.

When I started feeling drained and exhausted, just like my senior colleague then, I also began to feel unhappy. I would look at myself in the lavatory mirror on board and see a face of a person I did not know. The person who was once cheerful and fresh, full of life and zeal, was now staring at me with her puffy eyes and fatigued skin. Wrinkles that looked like craters. Pimples the size of a tiny *frais des bois*. And all that under the notoriously bright toilet light, which was anything but flattering, and which had a superpower to show the raw versions of you that you'd rather not see.

Then, I remember one day waking up early morning around 4 a.m. without having enough sleep, as usual. I jumped out of bed straight into preparing for my flight to Munich. And you know what my first thought of the day was? The big, comfy bed waiting for me in the hotel in Germany. While I was washing my face, I counted the number of hours I would have to work until I reached my hotel room and threw myself on the bed. I didn't think about sightseeing, walking, shopping or going to a nice restaurant. No, *the bed* was my number one priority.

Better said, my sleep was.

I wasn't aware of those thoughts for quite some time, but when that changed, it made my heart sink. It was clear that the pompous Brisbane lobby moment had arrived, and it was high time I planned my way out of flying.

Skybabe, my personal story isn't here to prove that all of us have an "expiry date" after ten years in aviation and that you'll have the same experience. I've seen people with over twenty years of flying experience have more life in them than some who are in their twenties and have barely passed over a year or two doing the same job. It all comes down to your personality and how much you love your job. How much of your energy you invest in it and how easy it is for you to regenerate and take care of yourself overall. It's all about finding that fine line between passion, enthusiasm, hard work, sleepless nights, skipped meals, and burnout. If you ever feel this way, just ask yourself, **what can I do to feel and look better?** Or, if you want to be radical, question yourself if you're still at the place where you really want to be.

These questions will help you decide:

- **Is what you're doing now worthwhile, even at the price of your health and well-being?**

- **Do you enjoy the actual job and all that goes with it (waking up at odd hours, interacting with people and colleagues, flying long hours)?**

- **What do you like about the job? What do you dislike?**

- **Are you learning new things? If yes, give three examples of the things you learned in the last month.**

- **Does your job lead to somewhere you want to go? Is it preparing you for something you might want to do in the future?**

- **Are you well compensated for the job you do?**

- **Does the job let you be creative and expressive of your ideas?**

- **How well do you integrate professional and personal life?**

- **What would you do differently if you could turn back time?**

- **Are you proud of the job you do and can openly talk about it, or do you shy away and don't want people to know what you do?**

ALL HAIL... ALICE IN ZOMBIELAND

I remember long ago, before we had all the fancy crew rest compartments with bunk beds, we weren't allowed to take a rest on board. So, imagine an eleven-hour flight to Japan where the only time you could relax was during your meal break. Sure, there were always a few smart colleagues who could skillfully sneak into the cockpit with a giant pillow from the First Class cabin, but if you were a junior who worked at the back of the plane, you weren't so lucky no matter how hard you tried. And for me, this simply wasn't something I would do out of respect for my senior colleagues and the flight crew.

Anyhoo, I was on my way to Perth, Australia, on a direct flight. I was excited to land on Aussie soil for the first time in my life. I'd dreamed of that country for so long that seeing this flight on the roster had me jumping up and down with delight, like Bambi enjoying the very first signs of spring. I made a plan to get to my room, take a shower, change and meet two of my colleagues with whom I had agreed to watch the Australia Day fireworks.

Of course, my intentions were one thing, but my brain begged to differ. I got to my room, mesmerized by the view from my hotel room window. With my suitcase and cabin bag out of my hands, I took my hat and jacket off and leaned against the window for a better look. The entire city smiled at me with its twinkling lights and endless skyscrapers. I checked the clock and gave myself a few more minutes of rest before I had to get ready and head downstairs.

A few HOURS later, a dazzling display of colorful fireworks woke me up. Yep, still standing, leaning my head against the window, in full uniform, I looked around, confused. I didn't even know I could sleep standing. How I managed to stay in one spot and not fall flat on my face is still a puzzling thought to this day. TRUE STORY.

IT GETS EVEN UGLIER

Another time I visited the land down under, I had one of those spectacular flights to Melbourne via half of planet Earth, with a three-day daily shuttle to New Zealand. By the time we finished the last three-hour shuttle, we all turned to zombies. The time difference didn't allow me to sleep, no matter how many chamomile teas I had before bedtime. On the third day and the final leg of our trip before going back home, I finally fell asleep with no memory of where I was. When I woke up, the clock read 6:30. I looked outside the window and saw a gorgeous sunset. Or was it sunrise?

Disoriented and in search of food to please my empty belly, I got out of the room and stopped a nice-looking lady on the street to ask what time of day it was. For a long moment, she studied me without blinking, probably thinking I was nuts.

But soon, she confirmed that, in fact, it was 6:30 in the evening. Another TRUE STORY!

Desynchronosis, more commonly known as jet lag, is real and *really* annoying, *Skybabe.* But it's the reality of the job and you must adapt. And with time, you'll become better at managing it.

31

You Decide Your Vibe

HOCUS-POCUS, ABRACADABRA OR SIMPLY PUT, ENERGY CLEANSE

*If you want to find the secrets of the universe, think
in terms of energy, frequency and vibration.*
Nikola Tesla

"Good morning Mr. Patel! Welcome aboard! Your seat is straight this way to the end."

"Morning Mr. White! How are you today? Straight and to your left, please."

"Hello to Almasi family. Welcome, welcome! Who do we have here? Hi Leila. Come, don't be afraid. You can hold my hand, you're okay. And baby Aisha. Yes, do not worry, we will provide a baby bassinet once we take off and the seat belt sign is off. You have four seats together, just behind the small galley in the middle."

"Good morning Mrs. Rossi. Hope you are well today! Yes, no problem at all. I'll send my colleague to bring some water for your medication immediately. You can wait here, please."

"Hi there, Marcio and Elena! Where are you two coming from, guys?

Oh, from Nepal! You climbed the Himalayas! Amazing! Well, it seems your backpack is a bit bigger than what's allowed in the cabin. Let's see what we can do about it. Give me a moment, please."

"Hi Marina, can you hear me? Yes, it's Nena. I've just boarded a gentleman in a yellow jacket who smelled of alcohol but I cannot confirm if he's intoxicated or not. He seems like he can walk and talk normally. I would like you to go to him with another colleague once he settles in his seat. Have a chat and call me back to give me your opinion, please. Yes, that one with a beard. Thank you. Gotta go. I have a river of people lined up in front of the door and I'm doing boarding on my own."

"Yes, Mrs. Li. It is very busy. Busy as usual. *Ni hǎo!* Welcome! The second right for you, please."

"Hello, Sadju, yes? What are you saying? Someone just fainted and Yukiko is giving oxygen to a passenger? It's too hot in the cabin, people are complaining? All right. Please, inform the Purser to adjust the temperature. I'll find someone to replace me here, and I'm coming to check on the fainting passenger."

And there it was. Just another ordinary flight, with me boarding around three hundred souls, mostly on my own.

The way my personality truly is and, plus, the way I was trained, obliged me to give my full attention to each person who stepped in and boarded the aircraft. And let's just stop right here for a second and acknowledge something. I said, "aircraft", not airplane. Something only *Skybabes* will understand. Our powerful, unique, and recognizable jargon.

Okay, now back to boarding!

To the person coming on board, I'd always give a genuine smile, try my best to pronounce their name properly, and make a friendly comment on their looks, clothes or shoes. In case I was inspired, of course. On flights to and from Italy and only a handful of other destinations, there was a lot of inspiration indeed. Wouldn't you agree?

I'd make jokes and have fun with passengers. I would observe them for medical and safety reasons, too. Or for the size of their bags.

This type of work requires **non-stop focus** from you, *Skybabe*.

And none of the passengers could ever tell I was doing zillions of things at once. That's called self-awareness and professionalism. Yes or yes?

Boarding is definitely the busiest part of the flight, and messing it up at the beginning could cost me a lot later. Therefore, I was paying not 100, but 200 percent of my attention to everything that was going on, and I would engage with as many people as I could.

A natural communicator who had no problem talking to almost anyone now had the chance to shine. *Voilà!* Strengthening tongue muscles at its best. Giving instructions to passengers and colleagues as a woodpecker. Repeatedly. Being constantly challenged by a variety and a number of issues coming up all at the same time made me think, decide, act swiftly, and become resilient to the bone. These not-so-common qualities I developed over the years, as I can say and see now, are the things I feel enormous gratitude for.

It's a well-known fact that we're always constricted by time, space, and resources once that aircraft lifts off the ground. But we do our best to use all that is available to solve passenger problems and make those flights safe and comfortable.

Before every flight, I'd decide that I would have a great one. No matter what happened and even if I felt like I just had the worst ten hours of my life, I still knew I would get back home safely with all the passengers who flew with me on that day. It was my inner talk and mindset that kept me safe and protected at all times.

Just remembering and writing about these experiences makes my head spin, but this scenario was the average of all the flights I'd done for the last six years of my flying, *Skybabe*. And as much as

I was known for my amazing and inexhaustible source of energy, I started getting tired. I was still doing my job, but it didn't feel the same. Over time, what looked scary or exciting to others became somewhat ordinary and maybe even boring to me. Like passing through a full cabin of passengers and yet—see no one, hear no one. If I chose not to.

It's like a special talent we, *Skybabes,* develop overtime for that horse-blinkers' phenomenon. We treat the aisle as the catwalk and nothing else is important but reaching those two destinations at opposite ends of the aircraft, with no obstruction or delay. As if humans around you don't exist at all. The funniest and the strangest feeling ever, you'd probably agree. Because they undoubtedly do.

Then again, don't forget those first few months of flying when you paid and gave your detailed attention to everything around you. The days where you felt so embarrassed and insecure about any new task that came your way. Whether you looked right, if you used the equipment correctly, or if you talked in an appropriate manner—every single thing mattered *then*.

Being flooded by rivers of heads moving up and down, left and right, staring at you, poking you, touching your uniform, asking, laughing, requesting, waving, sometimes even screaming—you name it—became your new reality. And, surprise, surprise, out of nowhere, you've found yourself on the theater stage without a single intermezzo with all eyes fixated on you until the end of every single flight. Unless, of course, you are in the lavatory. Okay, maybe also when you're on your break in the crew rest compartment.

It all sounds pretty exhausting and intense, doesn't it?

So, now you may wonder how to get away from all this. How to preserve energy, stay in a high-vibe mood and aligned from within? How to have the patience for that number of people and intensity of communication? Simply put, how to keep your sanity.

Well, here's the deal. The solution lies in finding that sweet spot where you answer to the demands of your job, but at the same time, you protect your personal boundaries.

The truth is, if you answered every single question, request, comment, and complaint, you'd easily get drained. Like a plant that hasn't been watered for months. Or, as my dear friend used to say in his cute Tunisian-French-Arabic English, "You end up living like a vegetable. You vegetate. You work and sleep and do nothing else". Dry and tired, with little energy left for yourself. Unless you are a cactus, of course. I'm not talking about being lazy and avoiding work. What I'm talking about here is that stage where you cannot handle it anymore—the pressure, the number of people, all the voices collectively asking something from you. You just want to tell them, "S-T-O-P! Have mercy, people!"

Your own cup becomes so empty and you need to refill it. It's your self-protection system—your energy preservation. Call it any way you want, but this is not about ignoring others, as some may think. This is about *you* and elegantly **preserving your peace.**

After many years, I realized one more important truth about my job.

Seemingly highly sociable to everyone around, flying can feel incredibly lonely. Such an irony. When your work requires you to be around people, you're surrounded by no less than hundreds of them constantly. But when your flight duty is over and you step into your hotel room, you're on your own—you with yourself in a big kingdom of *you*. Somewhere in some strange part of the world.

Let's just be clear here—I'm speaking in the name of the majority of *Skybabes,* not the exceptions who unquestionably exist and maybe want to prove me wrong. I'm talking about that feeling of putting your head on the pillow of some well-known five-star hotel where luxury stops being attractive and *wow.* Where you grab your phone with a wish to speak or send a message to a loved one, a friend or family member, but soon enough realize that they're fast asleep because the time difference between you is petty eleven hours.

Then the feeling of roaming the streets of a beautiful city in some faraway corner of the world, but having no one close to share that beauty and excitement with. Those moments, for sure, really felt lonely to me.

Although they can radically transform into so much fun if you have a good set of crew flying with you, most of the time you just have to learn how to deal with the solitude and make it comfortable for you. Because, the truth is, there is not much choice if you decide to take this job.

Learn to be your best friend, *Skybabe*.

Embrace the solo time and use it wisely. Recharge your batteries. Refill the emptiness with good energy and high vibrations, so you can show up as your best self in your life and on board. It's easier said than done, I admit, but I truly believe in these words and tips because they're the true essence of your well-being and taking care of yourself for life. I learned it the hard way and I'm still learning, I guess.

The truth is, I always wanted to give my all at work. I didn't save my energy. I didn't spare myself. I didn't know how to for years. Every request, every question, everything and anything I could attend to, I did. I had the most beautiful intention, but I would sometimes end up so depleted, even with tears in my eyes, because I was constantly absorbing all the energies that surrounded me. I didn't know how to handle it. Not all of them were good and there was no way out once you were in the air, stuck in that aluminum tube, either.

We are all energies and the moment someone steps in front of you, the first thing you notice, without even thinking, is how their energy feels. As they say, your energy introduces you before you speak.

Positivity expands easily, but negativity spreads like fire.

To illustrate it better, let me give you one juicy example out of many I had.

I remember two completely different flights, but with a similar issue we had on board.

Boarding was finished. Cabins were full. We were about to close the doors, but the flights kept being delayed. With the A/C not working, the temperature in the cabin kept rising and with each minute and full cabin capacity, passengers were getting anxious.

On one flight, people were understanding, calm, and patient. They listened to our instructions, ready to cooperate.

The other flight was a nightmare. The flight I wish I could erase from my memory. The passengers were impatient, collectively rude and inconsiderate that I felt like they would eat me alive. Bit by bit. Like hungry lions.

For the first time in my life, I was struck with so much negativity from a big group of people, so much pressure that was almost impossible to handle. I wanted to jump out of my skin. I still admire myself for being able to operate that particular flight in the end, but after I came home, I remember my breakdown, my tears, and sharing this story with my sister, who was visiting then. I couldn't take it anymore.

Falling apart, inside and out, I was ready to resign the next day.

And for the other flight—although the situation was identical, but on a different route—I received an award from the company, based on passengers' feedback. They expressed their gratitude for taking care of them and for handling the situation at the highest professional level.

See? Same, same, but different.

The bottom line is that cleansing and renewing energy can take many forms. You need to explore what works best for you, *Skybabe*.

32

Leaving Home, Heading Home

How to Plan Your Days

Life takes you to unexpected places. Love brings you
home.
Melissa McClone

Sugarplum,

You know the feeling.

Your alarm goes off, but the last thing on your mind is to get out of bed. You finally have that well-deserved day off, yet a few extra moments in sweet slumber won't make a difference.

Just ... one ... more ... minute.

Or a few hours.

I don't have a flight today. I can sleep for as long as I want.

Yeah, I get it. It's easy to turn around and continue sleeping. It's even easier to come up with an excuse and let your problems solve themselves.

Except, they won't.

Because you are the only one who can do this. You have the power within you to make a change and start living the life you've always dreamed of. Imagine having enough time to do all the amazing things you ever wanted to do on your days off. Yes, your days off are for resting and sleeping, but in between there is so much time you can fill your life with activities and adventures.

You deserve to wake up excited about life every single day, *Skybabe*.

And yes, you CAN do this.

What if I told you that there are amazing ways to get into the right mindset to achieve all the things you want? These simple actions will turn into powerful habits over time, helping you find creative ways to adapt to changes along the way and never give up on yourself.

So, let's dig in.

Plan Ahead

You get your roster in advance. Use this to your advantage. Plan your month ahead of time. When I first started flying, I had to plan my holidays yearly and everything revolved around those thirty days in a year with nothing in between. But as soon as I realized I was living from roster to roster, without the slightest idea what date or season I was in, I knew it was time for a change. So, I started planning my life according to what I wanted.

The beauty of making a plan is knowing exactly what to focus on. When you set your goals ahead of time, you have **something to look forward to,** and your mind knows exactly what to concentrate on the following day. You won't simply spend the whole day drooling on your pillow because you just came back from Brazil. **Get the rest you need, then live.**

Each month, when you get your roster, set aside half an hour to think about the things you want to accomplish the following month. Write them down in your *Skybabe* Journal together with powerful words of affirmation to motivate yourself to complete them. Use colorful pens, sticky notes, and motivational quotes. Whatever inspires you, do it.

So, let's say you schedule three tasks during your day off. To make sure you complete all three, choose the one you like the least and make it your number one priority. That way, you complete it first and once it's out of the way, the other two won't seem that difficult at all.

Go Outside

Always make an effort to leave your house, even if you don't plan to go anywhere that day. Go for a walk along the beach, meet up with an old friend, or go for a run in the nearby park. Share your thoughts with the people you care about. In return, listen to what they have to say and offer to hear their problems.

Just being out in the sun is a tremendous step forward to changing your mind and embracing happiness.

Write About Your Life and Your Travels

When you start building new habits, one of the best things to do is to keep track of your progress. And the easiest way to do this is to keep a journal. Write about your adventures, feelings, the people you meet. Write about what's bothering you and what you want to change in your life.

Take a Deep Breath

When life gets hectic and 24 hours seem too short to accomplish everything you have on your mind, take a moment to pause and just be. When you feel stressed and frustrated, just take a deep breath and relax. With all the distractions in your daily life, it's easy to forget to take time to appreciate and enjoy the surrounding beauty. Don't take little moments for granted. Make an effort to become aware and make them special. Schedule your downtime, drink from a fancy cup, wear your new shoes even if it rains. Watch the clouds, smell the roses, marvel at the full moon, sunrise, or sunset. Buy yourself all the stationery you desire, and indulge in nice pens and notebooks.

Skybabe, **what can you complete today that will make you happy when reflecting on your day?**

33

Congratulations, Skybabe!

You did it!

Yes, YOU, baby boo!

You have only yourself to thank for all the hard work, patience, and persistence.

We're so proud of you for coming this far, knowing how difficult it is to dedicate time to yourself and start working on bettering your life. We know it wasn't easy, but we hope you got a ton of value from this book and a giant spark of inspiration to continue to build your life the way you love and deserve! And all while flying!

Give yourself permission to enjoy the process, take risks, and make mistakes. This is the only way to learn. Remember that everyone's living their own story. Even those who are exceptional in some areas of life are likely struggling in other parts.

Whenever you try harder and still make a mistake, consider it a learning point and take away everything positive out of it.

Always allow yourself to be a learner. Trust that it's okay not to be perfect. With this incredible attitude, you'll inspire others to change their mindset and live better lives.

Remember:

Every time you break out of your comfort zone and start a new challenge, you're expanding your limitations. And when you successfully complete what you started out of your comfort zone, you're inevitably building confidence in yourself.

Leave room for new knowledge. Even if you think you know something well, open yourself to new experiences that will help you grow and prosper. There is nothing that can stop you. **You are your only limit.**

Gorgeous *Skybabe*, the more you know yourself, the better your life becomes. And the more you learn what you are all about, the more confident you'll feel. **Make every moment count.** Enjoy the job because it won't last forever. Someday you're going to look back and think of all the good things you went through. Bad things will dissipate and you won't even want to remember them. Now that you're there, high in the sky, or preparing to spread your wings, indulge in the moments this job brings you. And then, tell your story your way.

As you grow, you'll encounter new challenges and situations that will test your patience, self-esteem, and who you are. But you will grow through them, and you will learn from them.

Commit yourself to learning every single day of your life. Be consistent in studying, reflecting, and trying new things. Challenge yourself, take action, and get to where you want to go, one step at a time.

Taking small daily steps will make considerable improvements in the long run.

Life is what you make it. So, make it what you want it to be. You are confident, strong, and capable of doing anything you set your mind to.

And, at the end of each day, reflect and jot down:

- **What went well today, and why?**

- **How did you feel?**

- **What made your day?**

Then describe your day in just one word. If it is positive, indulge in your success. If it is negative, think of ways you can improve it and about what you learned.

To create and live a better life, you must allow yourself to have it. It's perfectly okay for you to have everything you desire.

Now go get it!

34

Not the Last Chapter

CALLING ALL SKYBABES

Holy bananas, *Skybabe*! You've made it to the end.

And guess what? There are no more questions for you to answer! *Whoop, whoop!* This was a heck of a journey, wasn't it?

Now, we want to hear from you and we want to publish your story! Wherever in the world you are and whatever capacity you work in as a flight attendant, please share your story with us.

Here are the deets:

- The story must be funny and deep, yet have a learning point.

- You must have some flying experience in the sky (as an active/retired flight attendant or a frequent flyer).

- Experience has to be your own (feel free to change the details such as names and destinations to protect the privacy of those mentioned in the story).

- Your story (include as many as you like and we'll choose the best one) has to be an event or a moment you experienced while flying (think of how it changed your life and what you learned from it).

- Any topic is fine as long as it relates to aviation.

- Include your Social Media handles (this is not mandatory, but we'd love to know who you are).

- We will never make major edits without your permission, but we do reserve the right to edit for things such as grammar, punctuation, spelling, and typos to make the story suitable for our next book. While we'd love to give you feedback on your writing, we will only inform successful *Skybabes* whose stories have been chosen for publication.

- If you're a *Skydude* and would like to be part of our journey, please send us your story. We'd love to hear from you, too!

- Email us a copy of the receipt that you purchased *Call Me Skybabe* book and, along with it, send us your story!

(callmeskybabe@gmail.com)

Write away! We can't wait to hear from you!

Thank You, Skybabe!

Thank you so much for taking the time to read our book! We hope you found the wisdom and inspiration you were looking for and that this little gem brought peace, clarity, joy, patience, gratitude, love, and courage into your life.

As much as we find it hard to say goodbye, we feel good knowing that we created something that changed the world for the better. Even if you found a spark of inspiration in one of our stories, we made a difference in your life, and knowing this makes us infinitely happy.

So, before we part, we want to ask you this:

Has anyone told you today how amazing you are?

Well, we want to be the ones who say it out loud so the entire Universe can hear it. Because we mean it.

We want you to know that you are beautiful. You are capable. You are everything you need.

We're so grateful for you and for having such a beautiful soul learn from our mistakes and experiences.

Now boo, don't let the world define you. The *Skybabe* you want to be is already within you. Let her lead you and show you that everything you've always wanted to be, do or have can be yours.

So, now that you've finished reading, please continue to journal. Set the intentions for the day and reflect on how your day went and what you learned. Make a conscious decision to write in your journal whenever you can, because it only takes a few minutes of your time, but it can leave a lasting impact on your life.

And don't forget to show yourself some love and positivity. Take the time to create daily self-love rituals that are just yours. Don't let anyone interrupt or take over your time. Give yourself a massage, blow yourself a kiss in the mirror with a big smile on your face, say to yourself that you are enough and that your body is a safe and happy place. ***Choose* to be happy.**

We wish you happiness and understanding, moments of revelation and awakening, and plenty of patience for yourself.

But above all, **we wish you LOVE.**

And finally, if you know *Skybabes* who need to hear words of encouragement and would benefit from reading these stories, please share our book with them.

Thank you.

With all our love,

Tee & Nena

Reviews Rock!

If you enjoyed *Call Me Skybabe* — **The Unfiltered, Laugh-Out-Loud, Empowering Guide to Finding Your Way to Health, Love, and Joy While Flying,** please leave a short review on Amazon or Goodreads.

Reviews help both readers and writers. They are a great way to support good work and help to encourage the continued release of quality content.

Please note: If you have questions or are interested in any of the courses mentioned in this book, send us an email and we'll connect you with the right people.

Skybabe Journal

Say hello to . . . your brand new, adorable *Skybabe* Journal!

Cute and pretty, our *Skybabe* Journal makes you want to pick up the pen and write whenever you see the charming, vibrant design. And it's made exclusively for you, *Skybabe*.

Plus, with a handy A5 size, it can slip in your bag easily, so you'll always get a chance to jot down your thoughts wherever in the world you are!

- Contains 150 pages

- Dimensions: 5.25 x 8 in (20.32 x 13.3 cm)

    To purchase your *Skybabe* Journal now, simply scan the QR code below!

About the Authors

Tee R. is a writer, certified life coach and teacher. For several years, she's helped women access their full potential, make transformational changes, and create balanced and fulfilling lives. As much as she loved coaching, Tee decided to give into her passion for writing and immerse herself in the world of fiction. Under a different pen name, she writes feel-good romance novels with zing, swoon, and a guaranteed happily ever after.

Having worked for a decade in different capacities for a renowned international airline, Tee knows what flying does to the body and how difficult it is to maintain a healthy lifestyle while changing time zones and hopping continents.

As an international scholar and teacher who's lived on four continents and has peeked into various corners of this majestic planet, she found an exceptional sense of freedom and self-appreciation while wandering.

In between parenting, traveling, and plotting her next novel, Tee is an avid reader and researcher who is passionate about protecting Mother Nature and preparing yummy vegan dishes.

·♥·♥· ♥·♥·♥·

Nena O. is a certified Holistic Health and Fitness Coach whose purpose in life is to inspire people to move better, lead a healthier lifestyle, and find happiness and beauty in the smallest of things.

From a true language lover and teacher who turned flight attendant with the entire world under her belt, Nena switched careers yet again and dedicated her life fully to wellness.

A devoted coach and a multi-passionate person, Nena lives and shares her passion for well-being. From teaching babies to swim, coaching women how to move, accept and love their bodies, instructing Zumba, yoga, breathing techniques, and fit box—to working with the elderly with various health issues—Nena covers it all.

Having the privilege of being exposed to such a diverse group of clients of different generations led her further to research the Blue Zones, secrets to longevity—a topic she's been excited about for the last few years.

When she's not coaching, teaching, dancing or organizing new travel adventures around the globe, you'll find her playing tennis on the beach, making delicious juices in her kitchen, or snorkeling with turtles along the pristine beaches of Mexico's Isla Mujeres.

By writing *Call Me Skybabe*, Tee and Nena connect health they often struggled with while flying and the world of aviation, where they spent over two decades of their lives together. They believe their unusual experiences and funny stories can serve as inspiration and a guide to other *Skybabes* who are already flying, have retired, or are yet to spread their wings in the sky.

Whether gorilla trekking in central Africa's rainforests on the slopes of the Virunga Mountains, sipping bubble tea in Singapore's Gardens by the Bay or hugging giant sequoia trees along the western slopes of the Sierra Nevada range, California, Tee and Nena continue to travel and hope to never retire their vagabond shoes.

Tee & Nena love connecting with their readers on Instagram @callmeskybabe or via email: callmeskybabe@gmail.com

Printed in Great Britain
by Amazon